THE PRESENCE AND ABSENCE OF GOD

THE CARDINAL BEA LECTURES

THE PRESENCE AND
ABSENCE OF GOD

Edited by
Christopher F. Mooney, S.J.

FORDHAM UNIVERSITY PRESS
NEW YORK

First published 1969 by
FORDHAM UNIVERSITY PRESS

PRINTED IN THE UNITED STATES OF AMERICA
BY THE COLONIAL PRESS INC., CLINTON, MASSACHUSETTS

To
Ruth Marie Hagedorn
Ecumenist among the first

CONTENTS

PREFACE

THE LECTURES PRESENTED HERE were delivered between 1966 and 1968 under the sponsorship of Fordham University's Cardinal Bea Institute. Founded in 1965 under the patronage of His Eminence Augustin Cardinal Bea, the Institute has as its general purpose to provide a forum on the university level where representatives of the Christian churches and the various academic disciplines can discuss the future of religious values in American life. More specifically, through a planned series of lectures and faculty seminars, it seeks to clarify the meaning of religious existence in a changing world and to search out new forms which the spiritual life may in the future be called upon to take. This is conceived as the task of a theology involved in active dialogue with the humanistic disciplines and with the natural and social sciences.

In cooperation with the theology department at Fordham, the Bea Institute provides interested doctoral candidates with an interdisciplinary program for the study of Christian spirituality. This program includes courses in the theology department touching upon the Biblical, historical and systematic foundations of spirituality, as well as courses in this and other departments dealing with the relevance of Christianity and non-Christian religions to western culture. In this way, it is hoped, what is proposed to the American Christian under the name spiritual life will receive serious academic scrutiny, and what is already being lived by believers will receive adequate theological expression.

These three orientations of the Bea Institute—interdisciplinary, interdenominational and interreligious—are being focused in the annual lectures series upon the general problem of atheism and its phenomena, including the dialectic of belief and unbelief within the Christian experience. This first collection represents the development of two principal themes, unbelief as a phenomenon in modern life and the problem of God as experienced by contemporary man. At times the primary concern of the lecturer is for the religious experience itself, at times for the mode by which this experience is conceptualized. In each case too there is an effort to take seriously the outlook of the unbeliever, for there is general agreement that unbelief is itself a witness that the meaning of God is a problem for the atheist as well, and that his testimony must challenge the Christian to a fuller articulation of his own commitment.

"Christian belief," writes Leslie Dewart, "finds in the conscious experience of lived existence both the absence and the presence of God." [1] A similar conviction underpins the thought of contributors to this volume, and it has led them to investigate, each through his own optic, the origins of the phenomenon in question, whether ethical, scientific, ecclesiological, sociological, epistemological or cultural. What has resulted is a series of bridges over the gap that separates the doctrine of God and the experience of man. The stress generally falls more upon the self-understanding of man as revealed by God than upon God's self-revelation to man. The theology herein is thus to a large extent anthropological; the questions men pose become more important than the answers they are able to give.

Shubert Ogden has well said that there must be an original confidence in the meaning and worth of life logically prior to every particular religious assertion. For only through such confidence do religious questions, not simply religious answers, first become possible or have any sense.[2] And this would seem to be the radical conviction behind the well-known diagnosis of Bonhoeffer, that God is now teaching us how we must live as men who can get along very well without Him. "The God who is with us is the God who forsakes us (Mark 15:34). The God who makes us live in this world without using Him as a working hypothesis is the God before whom we are ever standing. Before God and with Him we live without God. . . . God is weak and powerless in the world, and that is exactly the way, the only way, in which He can be with us and help us." [3]

PREFACE

Many people have been responsible for the success of these lectures. The writer is most grateful to the other members of the Bea Institute's executive committee who have shared with him the task of planning for the future: Dr. James M. Gustafson, Rev. Ladislas M. Örsy, S.J., and Rev. William J. Richardson, S.J. The numerous details connected with the lectures themselves were under the care of Mrs. Helen Zeccola, whose competence insured their efficient execution. But a special debt of gratitude must be acknowledged to Rev. Joseph P. Whelan, S.J., who originated the discussions leading to the foundation of the Institute, and whose advice and encouragement have been determinative factors in its subsequent development.

NOTES

1 Leslie Dewart, *The Future of Belief* (New York: Herder and Herder, 1966), p. 122.
2 Shubert M. Ogden, *The Reality of God and Other Essays* (New York: Harper and Row, 1966), p. 19.
3 Dietrich Bonhoeffer, *Letters and Papers from Prison* (New York: Macmillan, Paperback edition, 1962), pp. 219–220.

PART ONE

THE PHENOMENON OF UNBELIEF

CREATIVITY AND UNBELIEF

Robert O. Johann, S.J.

ONE OF THE MOST STRIKING CHARACTERISTICS of modern atheism is its pervasiveness.[1] It permeates the contemporary scene like the air we breathe. It is less (at least as I shall explore it) a fully articulated ideology than a mood or temper, a kind of presupposition, underlying contemporary man's efforts to come to grips with his world. Instead of being the conclusion of an argument, it is the implicit starting-point of a concrete way of life.[2]

This is at least part of the significance of the recent flurry about "death of God" theology. Whatever final importance one may attach to the phenomenon, and however much the "radical theologians" differ among themselves,[3] the broad, popular interest they have aroused bears witness to a widespread uneasiness and dissatisfaction with what has been known as religion. Instead of being meaningless on the face of it, the idea of God's death strikes a responsive chord in the hearts of a great many people, especially the young. The death of God would seem, as Vahanian suggests, to be a cultural event that has only to be pointed out to be acknowledged.[4] Even unacknowledged, the feeling is abroad that religion belongs to the past and that, whether or not God exists, a preoccupation with Him is an impediment to a truly human life.[5]

This is the point. Modern atheism is really a new humanism, bent on exploiting the potentialities of this life and stressing man's inalienable responsibility in this task. Hence its power and appeal. The negativity of getting along without God is only incidental to the driving and positive intention to live humanly. If modern atheism is aggressive, its aggressiveness is positively oriented. It is a full-scale campaign for a more human life with the accompanying notion that relying on God for this was, and remains, a mistake. Life can make sense only in the measure that man himself puts sense into it. To look to God for a happy ending is irresponsible superstition.

That such a mood should prevail to the extent it does would, I think, be impossible without the convergence in contemporary experience of two related factors: the living reality of belief as alienation, and the growing appreciation of intellect as creative. Neither, by itself, quite accounts for the present temper. As we shall see, creative intellect need not be interpreted atheistically. A theistic explanation of it is not only possible, but seems to be called for. If the case seems otherwise to contemporary man, it is because the creative ideal has emerged in a religious context that was—and continues to be—largely at odds with it. What concretely passes for belief in our culture too often involves a repudiation of intellect, an alienation of man from his deepest reality and responsibility as shaper of the world. On the other hand, the recognition of such alienation for what it is had to await the emergence of creativity. It is only in the light of a more human alternative that the distortions of current belief stand disclosed.

In the following pages, I shall try to trace out some of the relationships between these two factors and their bearing on contemporary godlessness. Since I take human creativity as open to another interpretation than that given to it by atheists who tend to understand themselves as its sole champions, it may be well to begin there. In the end, we shall have something to say about the connection between today's brand of atheism and authentic belief. For it may well be that, as Vahanian has suggested, the true line of demarcation runs not between atheism and theism but between idolatry and iconoclasm (both of which can be found among believers and unbelievers alike).[6] If that is the case, today's atheistic temper may seem less as a threat to the theistic stance than as an opportunity and a challenge.

I

However one may wish to interpret the fact, i.e., whether or not one sees it as a call to atheism, there seems little doubt that contemporary man finds his relationship to the world newly meaningful. He no longer sees the world merely as a place where he is putting in time on his way to somewhere else. It is no longer a testing-ground for life beyond the grave. Rather, the world itself has become the locus of man's fulfillment. It offers itself as a challenge to the full range of his creative powers. It is a wilderness to be tamed, energies to be harnessed, raw material to be converted into a genuinely human abode. Contemporary man no longer feels compelled, through ignorance or natural piety, to leave things as he finds them and put up with what he does not like. What he does not like, he feels called to change. His lot is not one of resignation and conformity to the existing state of affairs, however haphazard or irrational. His job, as he sees it, is to bring order out of disorder, to elaborate a city of man in which the previously random goods of experience are brought under control, made readily available, stable, and secure. The accomplishment of this task is both his own and the world's consummation.

The possibility of man's taking this active stance towards his natural and social surroundings and assuming responsibility for them depended on a number of conditions. For one thing, he had first to overcome his myopic view of time. So long as he remained ignorant of the past, he was naturally inclined to view the prevailing order in his world, whatever its limitations, not as something achieved historically, but as original, eternal and even divinely established. There was something absolute and sacred about the way things were—a conception which the Christian doctrine of creation actually tended to reinforce—

such that tampering with the given was felt as a kind of impiety. But once it became accepted that the present shape of things, far from being aboriginal, is the issue and upshot of an endless series of accidental convergences—in other words, a "happening"—the sacred aura surrounding the given was dissipated. The patterns of nature and society were desacralized and, in principle, were opened to change.

Another related condition for the widespread unleashing of reforming initiative was the radical weakening of the grip of tradition on individuals, which modern communications brought about. The communications explosion has prevented any single tradition from holding undisputed sway over communities and individuals alike. The questioning insecurity it has provoked—especially in those exposed to it in their formative years—has made doubt and dissent both widespread and respectable. The individual, as ultimate source of innovation, no longer feels obliged to conform to "the universally accepted" because this, even in appearance, no longer exists. The intellectual climate is volatile. However prone to routinization man remains, there is a general openness and respect for new ideas and practices, an attitude that is itself a novelty in the history of man.

But the central factor contributing to man's newly creative stance towards his world—and the one underlying the aforementioned changes in perspective—is the rise and triumph of modern science. Nothing has so profoundly affected man's understanding of the nature and role of his own intelligence as has the extraordinary success of his scientific endeavors. In the light of them, intellect can no longer be viewed as simply called to contemplate a real which somehow stands over against it, fixed and complete. It is itself involved in a process of real–ization, of giving reality itself a shape and direction it never had before. Rationality no longer means simply the capacity to recognize the reasons (*rationes*) of things and act in accordance with their requirements. It means even more profoundly the capacity to shape the reasons of things in accordance with the requirements of intelligence so that reason can

6

recognize itself in whatever it does. Correspondingly, the notion of meaning itself has been radically reinterpreted. Meanings have ceased to have the fixity of eternal essences. They have become temporal and dynamic. They are not originalities to which the mind can only conform, but eventualities in whose emergence the mind can actively conspire. They arise through the interplay of independent (i.e., not systematically related) centers of action whose potentiality for consequences, since it is a function of the endless variety of contexts into which they may be introduced, is indefinitely extensible. New meanings can, indeed, emerge by chance convergences. But once intellect is freed from its fascination with the actual, and turns instead to the deliberate exploration of the possible, the novel can be systematically and fruitfully pursued.

Dewey describes this new understanding of intelligence in the following terms:

The old center was mind knowing by means of an equipment of powers complete within itself, and merely exercised upon antecedent external material equally complete in itself. The new center is indefinite interactions taking place within a course of nature which is not fixed and complete, but which is capable of direction to new and different results through the mediation of intentional operations. . . . Mind is no longer a spectator beholding the world from without and finding its highest satisfaction in the joy of self-sufficing contemplation. The mind is within the world as a part of the latter's own on-going process. It is marked off as mind by the fact that wherever it is found, changes take place in a *directed* way, so that movement in a definite one-way sense—from the doubtful and confused to the clear, resolved and settled—takes place. *From knowing as an outside beholding to knowing as an active participant in the drama of an on-moving world is the historical transition whose record we have been following.*[7] [Italics mine.]

I have quoted Dewey at length, since it would be hard to find a more accurate description of the contemporary *attitude* towards intelligence. Admittedly, Dewey's interpretation has not won general acceptance among philosophers. Nor could the layman be expected to articulate his experience in precisely this fashion. But it is, I contend, what he *experiences*. Whether or not he knows it, he *lives* this view of mind, and he finds it satisfying.

In a sense, the scientific and technological experience of our age has provided contemporary man on the level of concrete life and practice with something philosophers in general have so far been unable to come up with on the level of theory. Erich Fromm has said that the great (theoretical) problem of today is the re-integration of man in his subjectivity and freedom with objective nature.[8] Past philosophies have not managed to do this. They have moved from the objectivism of the ancients (where man is integrated with nature, not in his selfhood, but only as a *kind* of being), to the subjectivism of the moderns (where the self, when it does not swallow nature, remains isolated from it), through the half-way house of medieval philosophy (which emphasized the person only to locate his fulfillment *as a person* in his relationship, not to nature, but to God).[9] But contemporary experience, which I think Dewey articulates well, has itself provided man with this integration. He now *experiences* himself as one with his world, not through objectivist conformity to its structures (which negates his selfhood), but through creatively transforming them (which gives him selfhood *in actu exercito*). At the same time that individual intelligence has been naturalized, the world has been humanized. There is a new at-homeness, a new wholeness, about man's relationship to his world—not that of a snug system, but rather that of an on-going *encounter* between independent initiatives (somewhat like a continuing conversation), which is at once a continuous challenge to inventive intelligence and a continuous consummation to the parties involved.

It is this wholeness of contemporary experience that lies in back of its immanentist interpretation. Contemporary man, for all the loose ends life may contain, does not feel obliged to look beyond it in order to make sense of it. Since, however, I have suggested that this new stance does not exclude a theistic interpretation, it may be well, before going any further, to sketch one briefly here.

II

Man's call to creativity is identically his experience of personal transcendence. The fact that man aspires to transform nature, to enhance his world, to move on endlessly beyond wherever he finds himself, is one with the fact that his nature is not-to-have-a-nature in the same sense as other natural entities. He is not so immersed in nature as to be imprisoned by it. As Scheler puts it, he is not condemned to carry his environment about with him "as a snail carries its shell." [10] He is open to more than the determinately actual, and can deal with things not merely in terms of what they are but in terms of what they may become, in terms of their possibilities. He is, therefore, not confined to the brute givenness of structures but is able responsibly to shape them. In a word, in his being and activity, man *transcends* whatever confronts him as actually patterned and determinate.

Because of this transcendence, an ethics conceived simply in terms of conformity to natural and social structures is necessarily inadequate. The fallacy behind much of the argumentation in favor of natural-law theory is that it mislocates the "nature" in question. The nature which can serve as ultimate norm for moral behavior is not that which confronts man as determinately structured; it is his own nature as a *reasonable* being, open beyond the given, and called to re–construct it in accordance with the requirements of intelligence. Thus a natural–law ethic is viable only if it is at the same time an ethic of reasonableness and personal responsibility.

But the question is: what does such reasonable responsibility imply? For the opponents of such an ethic argue that there are only two alternatives, conformity to patterns or subjectivist chaos. Nor could one answer them if beyond the determinate there were not the patternless-by-excess. In much the same way, Tillich's first two levels of courage, viz., that to be *as a part*, which involves a loss of self (objectivism), and that to be *as a self*, which involves a loss of the world (subjectivism), would exhaust the possible alternatives if, beyond beings, there were not Being itself.[11] In other words, an *openness beyond determi-*

9

nate structures is inconceivable (i.e., no openness at all) if it is not at the same time an *openness to what* is beyond the determinate. Nor is it enough to describe this "beyond" as the realm of possibility. On the one hand, possibility is rooted in actuality and, on the other, the order of determinate actuality cannot, by itself, provide the (ontological) space and ground for its own negation and surpassment. The realm of real and indefinite possibility thus necessarily occupies the infinite distance between particular beings and Being. Real possibilities are projected in the combined light of the determinately actual and the Infinite. In short, Being itself is inevitably ingredient in man's awareness of his own creativity. It is in Being's constitutive presence that he judges what is required for the world's enhancement. If someone objects that it is rather in accordance with the nature and requirements of intelligence that these judgments are made, the obvious answer is Yes—provided intelligence is viewed as the faculty, not merely of particularity, but of Absolute Being.

From this point of view, the thesis of Proudhon—namely, that humanity and divinity are first of all antagonistic, that the only way man can be himself is to banish the Intruder—is simply false. Actually, far from being at odds with humanity, the divine is what constitutes it. Man's very nature as a person is openness to God. His very essence involves transcendence. "Since this transcendence is not extrinsic but is intrinsic to man's being, not a dimension superadded to his life but rather as the ground condition for its possibility," [12] it is essentially ingredient in everything man does. All that is distinctively human, every perfection of man as man, is intrinsically structured by Being's creative presence and is finally intelligible only as a response to it.

An immanentist view, then, of human experience, based on man's new creative oneness with his world and the new wholeness which that has made possible, does not exclude a transcendental version. In fact, since the two are correlative, neither is really possible without the other. This does not mean that we call on God to fill up the holes in our lives or satisfy specific needs. The problematic in experience must be resolved—

in the measure it can be—on its own level. Since God is and remains beyond particularity, He abides forever on the far side of whatever solutions to our human perplexities we reach or fail to reach. He *is* the light which illuminates our search and measures all our achievements.

III

To say, however, that the reality of human creativity does not exclude the reality of God, that the contemporary ideal of creative humanism can be theistically interpreted, does not mean automatically that creativity is therefore compatible with theism as a way of life. For, as we pointed out, atheism today is less the conclusion of an argument than it is the premise for a style of living. The point is not whether the idea of God figures (as it does above) in a reflective interpretation of experience but whether the referent of that idea is to figure in any way in the conduct of one's life. In other words, can the idea of God have a real significance in the practical order without at the same time cramping and distorting that order? Can theism as a way of life be both significant and not dehumanizing? Today's atheist answers these questions in the negative. Looking at the history of religion, the record of man's attempt to translate the idea of God into practical terms, he contends that, where it has not been a record of downright inhumanity, it has at least fostered attitudes and practices that not only fail to give human intelligence its due but that run completely counter to the development of such intelligence.[13] The only times when this has not been the case is when religion has ceased to have practical import and become more a matter of lip service. But this last is simply hypocrisy and should be candidly confessed and eliminated.

Underlying atheist criticism of the religious record is a theoretical conviction that it cannot be otherwise. Putting it in its simplest form, one might articulate it this way: only the determinate and particular can have practical relevance, and nothing determinate and particular can be absolute. To absolutize the particular is superstition and idolatry; to refuse to particularize the Absolute is to deprive it of practical bearing.

11

Religion is therefore either dehumanizing or without significance, an impediment to human progress or a waste of time. Either way, man is better off without it.

Since this dilemma summarizes the main thrust of contemporary atheism *vis-à-vis* traditional religion, and since their growing awareness of this dilemma is at the root of much of the "agonizing re-appraisal" currently going on within the Christian communities, Catholic and Protestant alike, it may be well to explore it a little more in detail.

The force of the dilemma stems from the fact that it makes use of the very notion of transcendent Being which Western man has employed to articulate his understanding of divinity. If, for example, as Rahner writes, the primary "locus" of Christianity is the "transcendental experience which penetrates our understanding and our freedom as the unthematic ground and horizon of our everyday experiences" and which has as its focus "the incomprehensible wholeness of reality as its very center," that "absolute and holy mystery which we cannot seize but which seizes us instead, by its own transcendental necessity," [14] then it is clear that this constitutive presence of the Christian God can be reflectively grasped, *not directly*, but only through the mediation of signs and symbols pointing beyond themselves. Moreover, these reflective representations will be necessary if man is deliberately and socially to relate himself to this God, and to avoid an empty transcendentalism which, looking upon the transcendent as something elusive and unutterable, "advocates a program of so-called boundless openness to everything in general, together with a scrupulous avoidance of a straightforward commitment to anything in particular." [15] As Rahner continues, "These objectivizations [i.e., in human words, in sacramental signs, in social organizations] of God's own divine self-giving, which seizes man at his transcendental source, are necessitated by the fact that man must live out his original nature and eternal destiny as an historical being in time and space, and cannot discover his true nature in pure inwardness, in mysticism, and in the simple dismissal of his historical being." [16]

But then the difficulty arises. Either these objectivizations are confused with what they objectivize and are themselves given absolute weight, or they are not. If they are, religion is corrupted at its root. There occurs what even Christians are beginning to recognize as the unbelief of believers, a genuine atheism in their own midst. God is particularized and religion becomes a special domain. It consists in a specific pattern of behavior, with positive and negative elements. Conformity to this pattern is required if one is to be on good terms with the Supreme Being. Since this is what counts, a person may go through the prescribed motions (and consider himself a believer) without even holding that God exists. He behaves "religiously" just in case—as a kind of insurance policy.

But even if God's reality is held to, His particularity limits His bearing on one's life to the meeting of specific injunctions. Whatever lies beyond these is religiously neutral, i.e., to be dealt with as if God did not exist. Hence there are whole areas in the lives of "believers" where their religion makes no difference at all, where they are, quite simply, atheists. On the other hand, in the religious area, that of divine commands and prohibitions, they forfeit their humanity, since this area precludes any weighing of the merits of what is prescribed or forbidden in favor of blind conformity. They cannot behave intelligently, doing or avoiding something because of its inherent intelligibility or the lack of it; they can only behave slavishly.

This is what lies behind the atheist charge that objectivized religion inevitably involves an alienation from the human and creative. A particularized God is necessarily extrinsic to man, a kind of imposition from the outside. To bind oneself to such a God is to put oneself in bonds, to fetter oneself to a set pattern no matter what arguments can be raised against it. In this case, theism as a way of life is anti-human and atheism is a humanist revolt.

But suppose the objectivizations of God are not confused with the divine itself. Suppose they are taken simply as "mediations and signs of God's incomprehensibility," with their importance not in themselves but in what they make present to us. As determinate patterns and structures, these mediations are simply relativities. Only what they look to is absolute and that, as absolute, is indeterminate.

At this point, the other horn of the religious dilemma emerges with full force. For if only the Transcendent itself (and not as objectivized) puts an absolute claim on us, and if this claim is essentially indeterminate, then what practical bearing can it have on our lives? Once the objectivizations of God are relativized, are we not left simply with the absolute (but purely formal) demand to act intelligently in all circumstances? Can doing God's will ever be anything else than meeting the demands of intelligence? But then, why bother with all the religious paraphernalia? Indeed, there are good reasons for dropping them altogether. So long as the life of intelligent action is decked out in religious trappings, there is always the temptation not only to idolize these latter, but to attach a kind of divine importance to our own conclusions as well. Whatever course seems dictated by our intelligence, instead of being entertained modestly and as corrigible by future experience, will tend to be identified with the will of Being Itself, to become a kind of eternal law sanctioned by God, and so exclude further inquiry. Hence it seems better to many to drop all talk of God and simply concern ourselves wholeheartedly with the on-going process of "making and keeping life human." [17] As Dewey puts it, if we need a faith, let it be "faith in the method of intelligence," not as access to another world, but as a force for enhancing this one, the sole means we have for "rectifying and expanding the heritage of values we have received that those who come after us may receive it more solid and secure, more widely accessible and more generously shared than we have received it. . . . Such a faith has always been implicitly the common faith of mankind. It remains to make it explicit and militant." [18] This recommendation is being carried out today.

IV

From what has been said, it would seem that atheism as a way of life not only is compatible with a theistic interpretation of human creativity but can even be construed as demanded by it. Any effort to move theism from theory to practice seems bound to estrange us further from God's reality. This is why, as is often remarked these days, the atheist in his very atheism is, in a real sense, closer to God than those who "believe." If God is the ground of our humanity, He cannot but be authentically (even if only implicitly) affirmed in any affirmation of the genuinely human. By the same token, to the extent that what parades as belief diminishes or curtails our human capacities, it is just as really (however implicit) a denial of Him.

The question then arises: Even if one accepts the existence of God, is not an atheistic humanism perhaps the only authentic way to serve Him? Is there anything to be gained, for God or man, by diverting our attention from human and secular affairs in an effort to focus it on Him? This seems to me to be the decisive issue, and one calling for much more thorough treatment than I can give it here.

There are different ways to approach the question just raised —perhaps none of them wholly adequate in isolation from the others. I have tried to show elsewhere that the inherent ideal of the personal is a universal community of persons which can be conceived (and actually intended) only as a response to a transcendent Initiative.[19] In other words, the common recognition and celebration of God's reality is a prerequisite for the full realization of personal life. I have also suggested (along with many writers, to be sure) that only the communal acknowledgement of the Transcendent can keep man from worshipping idols.[20]

The point I would like to make here is that theism, not merely as a theoretical interpretation of experience but as a concrete way of orienting one's life, as a way of existing, is necessary if the humanistic ideal of creativity is not itself to become distorted. For, ingredient in the notion of creativity is the idea of man's own responsibility for the shape of the world. As Vahanian points out, far from proposing itself as something easier than the Christian ethic, the present-day atheistic ethic lays agonizing stress on individual responsibility and decision.[21] But, then, what does this responsibility entail? Does

15

it mean simply the assumption by man (individual? collective? both?) of the governance of his own life? Can one avoid aspects of responsiveness and answerability inherent in the notion of responsible behavior, or not ask the question: To whom is one responsible?

When God is eliminated as ultimate focus of one's practical orientation, it would seem impossible to keep creativity from degenerating into either a kind of Sartrean subjectivism or a levelling collectivism. If intelligence is simply a private endowment, then in my efforts to meet its requirements, I am answerable only to myself. If it is, on the other hand, essentially a communal affair, so that it is in terms of common approbation that its determinations are validated, then we do indeed move beyond subjectivism—the individual is now answerable to others, to the group—but we also fall under the tyranny of "what is commonly accepted." In other words, it would seem that only a thematization, in practice as well as theory, of the responsive and responsible openness of intellect to the Transcendent Other as its own ground can save the ideal of creativity from falling into either of these traps.

A practical recognition and celebration of God's presence to us need not mean diverting our attention from human concerns to fix it elsewhere; it is, I would maintain, essential to meeting those concerns in a fully human way. As here entertained, however, God is not the invisible hand shaping events nor the Supreme Quarterback calling all the plays. He is not to be looked to as the Source for specific directives or solutions. The working out of these is the task of human intelligence. Nor can God be called on to sanction the plans or programs we come up with. Neither issuing directives nor sanctioning complacency, God's presence continually summons us, whatever our accomplishments, to the task of intelligent action and calls all our achievements into question. It is the recognition of our responsibility to God, of the fact that intelligence is our responsive encounter with Being itself, that puts our whole life and all our deeds under judgment and prevents us from ever giving our final allegiance to anything finite, be it ourselves or the work of our hands. In God's presence we are never so just that we are not also sinners, never so sinful that the path to redeeming our past is closed. Thus, instead of being antagonistic to our humanity, God is its deliverer, its liberator. He frees us from the isolation of our own subjectivity while excluding our absorption by the collective. On the other hand, as judge of our collective efforts, He frees us from a slavery to our past, from thinking our communal structures to be any more than temporary improvisations in continual need of correction, from every ideology that would reduce our collective selves to a homogeneous mass, including those ideologies of intelligence, scientism and technologism.

Needless to say, God is all this for us only when the cultural embodiments of His presence allow Him to be so. Religion, as a cultural achievement, stands as much under God's judgment and is as continually in need of reform as anything else. That past religious traditions have not infrequently obscured God's liberating significance goes without saying. Nor is this the place for a discussion of how they might be revised. The point is that if God is really the One who frees man to build his world and become himself in the process, then there are not a few, still standing, religious idols that must be tumbled to make room for Him. And if this is the case, then present-day atheism is not without positive religious import. By iconoclastically espousing the cause of human freedom and creativity, it has awakened the religious conscience from complacency to an ashamed awareness of its own shortcomings. Though not itself the full answer to man's plight nor a wholly reliable herald of salvation, it has, nevertheless, by concentrating on the meaning of man, thrown no little light on the meaning of God.

NOTES

1. Cf. M. Marty, *Varieties of Unbelief* (New York: Holt, Rinehart & Winston, 1964), especially the chapter on "The Originality of Modern Unbelief."
2. Jean Lacroix, *The Meaning of Modern Atheism* (New York: Macmillan, 1965), p. 8.

3. Cf. Rosemary Reuther, "Vahanian: The Worldly Church and The Churchly World," *Continuum* 4 (1966), pp. 50–62, esp. 50–51.
4. This is the pervasive theme of G. Vahanian's *The Death of God: The Culture of Our Post-Christian Era* (New York: Braziller, 1957).
5. See A. Dondeyne, "Les leçons positives de l'atheisme contemporain" in *Il Problema dell'Ateismo* (Brescia, 1962); also J. C. Murray, "On the Structure of the Problem of God," *Theological Studies*, 23 (1962), pp. 1–26.
6. Cf. G. Vahanian, "Swallowed Up by Godlessness," *The Christian Century*, December 8, 1965, pp. 1505–1507, esp. 1507.
7. John Dewey, *The Quest for Certainty: A Study of the Relation of Knowledge and Action* (New York: Putnam, 1929), pp. 290–291.
8. As reported by F. Parker in "The Temporal Being of Western Man," *Review of Metaphysics*, 18 (1965), pp. 629–646, esp. pp. 632–633, and based on Erich Fromm's *Escape from Freedom* (New York: Holt, Rinehart & Winston, 1960).
9. A similar interpretative scheme is developed by F. Parker in his "The Temporal Being of Western Man," cited in n. 8. See also my *The Pragmatic Meaning of God* (Milwaukee: Marquette University Press, 1967).
10. Max Scheler, *Man's Place in Nature* (New York: Farrar, Straus & Giroux, 1961), p. 39.
11. Cf. Paul Tillich, *The Courage to Be* (New Haven: Yale University Press, 1962).
12. K. Rahner, "Christianity and Ideology," in *The Church and the World, Concilium*, Vol. 6 (Glen Rock: Paulist Press, 1965), p. 51.
13. See, for example, Dewey's criticism of traditional religion in his *A Common Faith* (New Haven: Yale University Press, 1934).
14. Rahner, *art. cit.*, p. 50.
15. *Ibid.*, p. 43.
16. *Ibid.*, p. 45.
17. Cf. Harvey Cox, *The Secular City* (New York: Macmillan, 1965), p. 255.
18. Dewey, *A Common Faith*, p. 87.
19. Johann, *The Pragmatic Meaning of God*.
20. Johann, "Creativity without Guilt," *America*, August 14, 1965, p. 165.
21. Vahanian, *The Death of God*, p. 185, p. 193.

FAITH, UNBELIEF AND MORAL LIFE

James M. Gustafson

A SEMINARIAN RECENTLY CAME INTO MY OFFICE, and with great passion said, "Mr. Gustafson, the issues are so visceral, and you're so damned cerebral!" In a sense his comment, which I take not to be untypical of this generation that wills to be where the action is, provides a text for what follows. It is not that I accept it as an accurate description of my own view of moral life, but I shall use it as an expression of a view of moral life that pervades many of the younger students whose courage and deeds I deeply admire.

This seminarian's comment seems to suggest a number of things. He trusts his moral sensitivities, his profound feelings of compassion, his sense of injustice, his activated will, his moral responses that involve his deepest emotions. He is suspicious of moral ideologies that rarify religious or moral beliefs; he is suspicious of ideologists who assume that they have done something for the well-being of man when they have refined and stated the doctrines and dogmas they believe to be true and correct. He is suspicious of preoccupation with ethical reflection that makes distinctions between teleological ethics and deontological ethics, between different approaches to the logic of moral decision-making that spins theories about the relation between intellect and will, between intention and action, between fact and value. In short, he is suspicious of *beliefs*, but

about abstract justice or abstract love. We realize that we are moved by a deep longing of the soul, by a profoundly inward desire, when we seek peace and freedom for all men.

We know that Christian morality has love as its primary form, and we know that love is never reducible to an idea about love. We know, with Bernard Häring, that Christian morality is a "dynamic morality of love," that love is a power as well as principle, that love requires heedless self-sacrifice as well as the cool reflection of the virtue of prudence, that love claims and moves us sometimes to do more than, and sometimes other than the civil law requires. We are both emancipated from the past and moved toward the future by the conviction that the Christian life has as its law the dynamic presence of God's spirit working in and through us and in and through the events to which we respond. We are convinced that the law of the spirit of Christ and the empowering and authorizing principle of love bring a vitality and freshness that the stale thoughts and moral laws of men have long ago smothered.

If we can use the word *belief* to point to intellectual assent to moral and doctrinal ideology, to credence and to a prizing of the activity of the intellect in explicating and refining moral and doctrinal distinctions, ours is surely a generation of *unbelief*. It is not so much that there is an aggressive antagonism against doctrines, as if a movement had to be organized to abolish some if not all of them. It is more that they have the appearance of unreality, of insignificance, of irrelevance. Indeed, for some of us, they would simply wither away from ineffectiveness and disuse like the tail withered away on the erect vertebrate called man, if there were not institutions seemingly dedicated to keeping doctrines and principles alive.

If we can use the word *faith* to point to a profound consent of the will, to a personal reliance of man's whole being, to involvement and commitment, to loyalty, ours is a generation of *living faith*. There is a confidence (at least on some days) that man is for the future and the future is for man. There is a "gutty" hopefulness that we sometimes feel without having to justify it with doctrines about the Kingdom of God which will come, or about the Omega point that draws all things to a fulfilled and loving future. There is a reliance upon both the goodness of life and upon the capacity of free men to realize it that does not ask for explanation about why life is good, or how man's freedom is to be interpreted. We *trust* in the good ness of life, we trust in freedom, we trust in love. There is no burning interest among many of our contemporaries to articulate *beliefs* about the goodness of life, beliefs about freedom, beliefs about love.

But now some questions have to be asked. What is the relation between the cerebral and the visceral? What is the relation between moral beliefs and moral actions? What is the relation between articulated religious convictions and profound religious trusts? Is there an intrinsic connection between them so that my *knowledge about* values, about the goodness of life, about the right, has some effect upon what I value, how I respond to life, and how I act? Or are we faced with a disjuncture, an unfathomable gulf between formed beliefs and living faith, so that belief does not inform and direct trust and action? This is a generation that is very sensitive to the dishonesty, insincerity, inauthenticity and phoniness of the observable discrepancy between what men say they believe in, and what they obviously really trust in and obviously really do. Is the disjuncture a necessary one? Or is it an accidental one? Or is it one that points not to the irrelevance of belief, but to the moral failure of men? Can we have trust without some conviction about that in which we trust, some belief about that in which we have faith? Are there not unexplicated beliefs, implicit beliefs in our trusting personal lives? Is it not the case that unless we articulate and examine critically the things in which we trust, that we are likely to be deceived by ourselves and others about their reliability, their validity?

Such big questions, which consume the energies of philosophers and theologians, cannot be answered here. But I would like to approach an answer by beginning with experience and practice, and working somewhat inductively from it. For instance, when someone tells me that he knows what he is doing is right because he feels that it is right, I like to have time for extended conversation with him. I cannot tell him that

23

I am sure that what he is doing is morally wrong simply because he is relying upon his feelings to validate it. He may indeed be more perceptive, more helpful, closer to the bullseye of the moral target than those who work with great deductive skill from universal moral propositions to the particular case in hand. But I would like to ask him if his assurance that his action was the right one was based *only* on his feeling of its rightness. If he says that it is, that he senses in his bones that it is right, then I have to ask another question. I have to ask how he would judge between his act and its feelings and the act of another man who does what is opposed to his act, but also is validated by feeling. This is to bring the moral discourse to a certain objectivity, to find out what things other than feeling would determine, between two judgments and actions, which was better and which was worse. Perhaps both a member of the John Birch Society and a member of the New Left would say that they feel deeply the rightness of their respective causes. But something else than their feelings would be involved in the determination of their allegiances and conduct.

My "someone" is likely to provide some reasons either for trusting in *his* feelings but not trusting the other man's feelings; or reasons why his action, because of its consequences or because of the principles which govern it, is better than the other man's. My "someone" may say that one has to go behind feelings to find out what generates and informs them, if he wills to defend his feelings against another man's. He might claim that his have a moral validity because he has had a wider experience than another man has; his are tested in the crucible of moral seriousness, of experience of injustice, of involvement in action, of suffering. To this I might respond: you not only *believe* that feelings are trustworthy, but you *believe* that moral feelings are engendered by *experience*, and that some experiences are more appropriate than others in order for proper moral feelings to be engendered. I could press for articulation and defense of these implicit, unexplicated beliefs, not for the sake of sophomoric dialectic, but for the sake of clarification of what my "someone" *trusts* in, and *why* it is trustworthy.

If my "someone" does not want to show why feelings and particularly his feelings are morally reliable on the basis of an inward introspection, he may tell me that the authentication of his feelings is *in the consequences* of the actions that expressed those feelings. We can see quite simply, however, that he now will be asked why those consequences are good. He may say they are good because injustice has been rectified, or that suffering has been relieved. What would he say if I asked him why injustice ought to be rectified, why suffering ought to be relieved? He might say different things. He might say that it is self-evident that injustice and suffering are bad, and what relieves them is good. And I might ask, "Why is it self-evident?" This could be pursued, if his patience permitted, to the point where he might have to declare that he *believes* that all men have an inclination to abhor suffering and injustice; he believes something about human nature not only to be true, but to be important in the determination of conduct.

Or he may say his actions are good because his feelings are loving feelings and because he trusts in love. Let us assume my "someone" has a traditionally Protestant turn of mind, and answers my query about *why* love is trustworthy with this: "because the Bible says so, and because the Bible says that God is love." He is stating some things about what he trusts in (he trusts in what the words of the Bible say), and he is opening up the way for an intellectual defense of that in which he trusts. Thus we can examine with some objectivity what it is upon which he relies, and we can compare it with other possible convictions. But what have we achieved? A scintillating conversation? Not just that. We have hopefully achieved clarity. But is clarity important, and if it is, why? It is important because it aids one in examining his conduct and moral being. It helps one to judge himself, and to be judged in the community of which he is a part, not as if this earns him grace and merit, but in order to live with greater moral effectiveness and accuracy.

What generalizations about the significance of beliefs can be extrapolated from my hypothetical discourse with my "someone"? I would like to cite four interrelated points.

First, clarity, while not the exclusive value in life, is nonetheless of great importance. Self-consciousness of what one trusts in, what one relies upon, what one values, what one desires, leads to more accurate self-understanding, sharpens one's awareness of who he is. I am not talking about the formulation of an ideal self-image, nor about a self-image that can be marketed when the representatives of industry come to interview you for prospective employment. I am talking about accuracy in one's perception of what he is, what his words and deeds express and represent, what values and convictions give him that measure of moral wholeness, consistency, and integrity that he has. If I do what I deeply feel like doing, then it is worth knowing that I am one who trusts in his feelings, that my integrity is based upon such consistency as my sensibilities and affections have. This self-knowledge, based on articulation of what seem to be the objects of my loyalty and trust, in turn affects my further responses.

Second, bringing objects of loyalty and trust to articulation, to a stage of assertions of beliefs, enables me to examine myself. In the light of what do I examine myself? In the light of a normative understanding of what I am, or what I ought to be; a normative understanding of what ends I ought to have, what deeds I ought to be doing. Even in the best of men there is often a discrepancy between their highest and best intentions and the ruling desires and impulses that govern their actual behavior. There is an abrasiveness between a normative self-image and normative self-understanding on the one hand, and the actual portrait one might induce from critical reflection upon one's actual objects of trust, one's actual values. As Socrates taught long ago, the unexamined life may lead to self-deception, as well as to deeds that miss the mark. One can ask himself whether what he really trusts in is worthy of the trust that he has in it.

Third, the formulation of our trusts into assertions of belief enables us to engage in critical comparative scrutiny of alternative objects of trust. If, on the basis of self-examination I find that on the whole I live according to the demands made upon me from one occasion to the other, with a kind of other-directedness, I can ask myself whether I really believe in an occasionalism that takes its signals from others. I can subject an occationalist view of life, an other-directed view of life to greater objective scrutiny. I can find from literature, philosophy, biographies, or personal acquaintances that there are options to the kind of beliefs I seem to have. These can be examined comparatively; judgments can be made about the alternatives; I can see whether my values, my beliefs can stand critical scrutiny in the light of these alternatives. No one can claim that we choose our objects of trust simply on the basis of relatively objective discourse about alternatives; there is always a deeply subjective aspect to moral life, a sense of allegiance and commitment that has the mark of a leap, a choice, a more than rational trust. But the beliefs by which we live can be subjected to comparative critical scrutiny, and within limits new choices can be made, and old allegiances revised.

Fourth, in this process of clarification both of what we really live by and what we can or ought to live by, our chances of greater moral accuracy are improved. Just as we are more likely to meet the deepest needs of a particular neighbor if we know that neighbor well, so we are more likely to do what is for his well-being if we are reasonably clear about what human well-being consists of. Just as our social action is more likely to be effective if we understand the social dynamics within which we exercise our influence and power, so it is more likely to achieve the human good if we are clear about the ends to be sought, the justice or the mutuality to be brought into being. Articulated and examined beliefs about justice help us to discern what the just act is in a particular place, just as they help us to see what the state of affairs we are seeking to bring about in that place really is.

Moral passions, visceral responses are based upon objects of trust; the cerebral can bring these to consciousness. The visceral moral man needs to examine himself; his cerebral activity can help him to see the inconsistencies and discrepancies between what he is and what he wills to be. By bringing the objects of trust to the articulation of beliefs, the cerebral can engage in the comparative examination of alternative values and beliefs. And beliefs articulated and examined by the cerebral can give direction to responses that are also deeply visceral. Moral faith without moral belief is blind; moral belief without moral faith is powerless.

What does all this have to do with Christian morality? First, it helps us to see that Christian morality is not unique and esoteric by virtue of being a morality of trust and belief. There is in each man's moral life a post-ethical commitment, a confidence and a trust in some values, some beliefs, some persons, some communities, some desires, some affections. The phenomenon of trust, of faith, is a human phenomenon, present in everyman. Implicit convictions, if not explicit beliefs are present in the behavior of every serious moral being. Christian morality is not unique because it is a morality of trust; it is not unique because it is a morality of belief. What distinguishes the morality of the Christian community is its *object* of trust, its affirmations about the One in whom it trusts. What distinguishes the morality of the Christian community is the root and ground of its moral faith, its allegiance to Christ as the One who has come to disclose to all men that the Ground and Giver of life is Good, that in its creation and in its newness of life God wills the well-being of His creation. Christian morality is an expression of a trust in the goodness and power of God, the creator and orderer, and redeemer of life; a goodness made known in the advent, the birth, the words and deeds, the death and the new life of Jesus Christ.

Second, we can see how the moral perspective and posture of the Christian community can and ought to be empowered, governed, and formed by the trust of its members in the goodness of God. Because of our trust in the power and goodness of God, we can and ought to act in a spirit of confidence and hopefulness, knowing that the One who has brought us to our time and place, and the One who meets us as we respond to the openness of the future is One who sustains and wills the well-being of all men. Because of our Christian trust, we ought to have the courage to risk something of ourselves, and something of the past that we cherish, for the sake of finding the deeds that are fitting both to the God in whom we trust, and to the needs of man in the world. Because of our Christian faith, we ought to be lovers of mankind, lovers of the life that God has given, lovers of the good. The attitude, the perspective and stance of Christians can and ought to be consistent with, congruent with the One in whom they believe.

We can see how trust and belief belong together in Christian morality. Apart from belief, apart from assertions that point to God through Jesus Christ His Son, we would not see as clearly as we do (in trust and in hope) that God is worthy of our trust, our hope, and our love. Apart from trust we could not have that perspective and stance, that attitude toward others and the world that is the human heart of Christian morality.

Third, we can begin to see how our moral *judgments* and *actions* are formed and informed by both our trust and our beliefs. Our moral deeds are expressions of our affections and sensibilities as these are nourished by our trust in the goodness of God made known in Jesus Christ. We can and ought to be sensitive to the victims of injustice and poverty, of war and natural disaster without being reduced to globs of sentimentality. We ought to have a sense of indignation without perverting it into sheer rebelliousness. We ought to make our choices in our hope without being subject to illusions. We ought to take delight in the moral goodness of the world, and affirm it in our words and deeds without clutching it to ourselves as if it were ours to possess. We ought to be able to be humble without hating ourselves, to be joyful in our moral lives without being shallow. And yet our judgments and deeds are not just the expressions of affections and sensibilities nourished by our trust in the goodness of God.

Our judgments and deeds can and ought to be congruent with our beliefs about the One in whom we trust. Belief in God's disclosure in Jesus Christ can form and inform the ends that we seek in our deeds. Consonance rather than dissonance with the purposes made known and fulfilled in Him can and ought to be the objective of our moral acts and deeds. Not consonance with Christ as the be-all and end-all in Himself, but consonance with Him in order that we might be ourselves agents bringing newness of life into being, bringing moral good out of moral evil, serving the well-being of man. Our words and deeds in human relationships, in the exercise of political rights and power, in the important and unimportant things of life can and ought to have a coherence and integrity formed by our convictions about what God has done and seeks to do for man in and through Christ His Son. Beliefs give us direction, beliefs shape our ends and intentions, beliefs become norms for guidance in our judgments and deeds. Our discernment of what we ought to say and do, of what we ought to be, can and ought to be formed both by our trust and our belief in Christ, the One in whom God has made Himself known. Both visceral sensitivity and rational discrimination are part of Christian morality; both are grounded in Christ. God's gracious initiative in giving and renewing life gives and renews our spirits and our minds.

Someday I shall meet my seminarian in the hall, and passionately say, "Mr. Seminarian, the issues of moral life are awesomely visceral and awesomely cerebral." I shall say, "It is worth articulating those things in which you trust, it is worth examining your profound feelings." I shall say, "Judge those beliefs, judge those feelings, and use both in your discernment of what you ought to do." I shall say, "Trust and belief are two sides of one relationship: to God and to your neighbor." I shall say, "Faith in God is faith in a God who has made Himself known. We can trust Him because we have beliefs that disclose Him to us." I shall say, "Christ not only gives us a newness of life on which we can rely, but He is for us the pattern of our reliance and our deeds." I shall say, "Faith without belief is blind; belief without faith is powerless." I shall say, "Moral man is both visceral and cerebral; moral action requires both trust and belief."

TEILHARD DE CHARDIN
ON BELIEF IN GOD

Christopher F. Mooney, S.J.

In his book, *No Other God,* Gabriel Vahanian notes with a perceptive accuracy that

The vulnerability of the Christian faith hinges today on the fact that there can be no faith in God which does not assume a concomitant cultural obligation. There can be no faith without secularity. . . . Should, then, the Christian faith be unable to overcome its present cultural estrangement . . . its only alternative is to become an esoteric mystery cult, that is, the very antithesis of what it has claimed to be for twenty centuries.[1]

What I wish to underline in the pages that follow is that a major preoccupation in the writings of Pierre Teilhard de Chardin is precisely to overcome the present cultural estrangement of the Christian faith. His efforts, made over a period of forty years and bridging two world wars, have in the course of time reflected the growing concern of an ever larger number of Christians. The recent *Constitution on the Church in the Modern World* is sufficient indication, I think, that the Second Vatican Council addressed itself to this problem. It says:

The People of God labors to decipher authentic signs of God's presence and purpose in the happenings, needs and desires in which this People has a part along with other men of our age. For faith throws a new light on everything, manifests God's design for man's total vocation, and thus directs the mind to solutions that are fully human. . . . This Council wishes to assess in this light those values which are most highly prized today, and to relate them to their divine source.[2]

No one surely was more conscious of these "happenings, needs, and desires" of our age than Teilhard de Chardin. Nor was anyone more anxious than he to find therein "authentic signs of God's presence and purpose," so that the unbeliever might see how Christian faith "directs the mind to solutions which are fully human." It was indeed through this double effort that he sought to overcome the present cultural estrangement of Christianity, and he developed as a consequence a dialectic on the problem of God oriented toward the temporal as well as toward the eternal. Nevertheless, it must be insisted upon that for Teilhard the problem of God was initially a personal problem. What he always fell back upon was his personal experience. It was this experience of a hidden God, who remains hidden even when experienced, which convinced Teilhard that he had a message for modern man. This message was a double one: man's need for an absolute and man's need for Christ. These two needs Teilhard had himself experienced in and through his commitment to science and contemporary culture, and he believed that an analysis of the evolutionary process could help modern man to recognize these needs also in himself. To document, then, Teilhard's contribution to current discussion on the phenomenon of unbelief, we shall briefly outline the problem as he experienced it personally and then indicate how he developed his own double answer.

I

Everyone today is aware that Teilhard's fundamental problem of life was a clarification of the relationship between the world which he had discovered through science and the God whom he had experienced through faith. He lived too close to the modern unbeliever not to be vividly aware of the possibility of living a fully human life without any concern for God at all. The humanist with whom his scientific work brought him into daily contact inevitably possessed a profound respect for the dignity of man, as well as an enthusiasm for his exercise of freedom and his responsibility to build a better world. His moral ideal, moreover, was usually quite high, his dedication to his work total, and his commitment to the values of technological progress sufficiently strong to motivate his life. Teilhard once wrote:

There is a certain pessimism about, which keeps repeating that our world is sinking into atheism. But shouldn't we rather say that what it suffers from is an unsatisfied theism? You claim men no longer want God. But are you certain that what they are rejecting is not simply the image of a God too small to nourish our concern for survival and for a super-life, which is, after all, nothing else than our need to adore? [3]

And in another essay we find a remark which Teilhard said he had heard many times from unbelievers: "Were I to become a Christian, I have the impression I would be diminishing my-self." [4]

We accept as commonplace today that modern secular man finds it impossible to ask questions about God or Christianity in other than human terms. But Teilhard saw this clearly many years ago, at a time when it was recognized by relatively few Christians and admitted by almost none. He wrote in 1949:

For a reason that is not clear, something in our time no longer "clicks" between man and God, as God is presented to him today. Everything seems to point to the fact that man has no clear picture of the God he wants to adore. Hence the general impression . . . we get of an irresistible growth in atheism.[5]

Such a growth, however, he felt to be only apparent. The heart of the problem was that God was now being experienced less in a religious and more in a cultural context. This was, he admitted, still an obscure experience, but nonetheless real and nonetheless to be valued. "However worthy of condemnation many of the forms assumed by 'faith in the world' may be, they derive from an undeniable effort to be loyal to life (that is to say, to God's creative action), and this we must respect." [6] Teilhard was conscious of having a very intense awareness of

33

the aspirations deep at the heart of his age as other men seem to have of its miseries.[7] Destiny placed him, he said, at a privileged crossroads, where it was possible for him, in his double role as priest and man of science, to experience the interplay of two powerful currents, the one human and the other divine.[8] The following text, taken from an important essay written in 1934, makes this clear:

After thirty years devoted to the pursuit of interior unity, I have the impression that at last a synthesis has taken place naturally between the two currents which draw me. Each has in turn strengthened, not diminished the other. Today I probably believe more than ever in God, and certainly more than ever in the world. Is there not to be found here, on a small scale and at least in rough form, the personal solution of the great spiritual problem which today confronts the vanguard of humanity? . . . Even understood in purely subjective terms, much of what I say must necessarily have an equivalent resonance even in temperaments unlike my own. Man is essentially one, and it is sufficient to go deep enough into oneself to find a single common ground of aspiration and insight.[9]

This last text makes it clear that Teilhard felt not only that his own problem was that of modern man generally, but also that his personal solution had, at least as a rough sketch, a universal validity.

The problem of God today confronts the whole spectrum of human activity. We can come to grips with it only by using all the resources of research and human experience. Not only does God give a value to human effort which will last forever, but his revelation is precisely a response to the sum total of this effort.[10]

In his own life, then, Teilhard had found a coherence between his faith in God and his faith in the world, and their meeting point was the broad support given by Christianity to human endeavor and to man's aspirations and hope for the future. At the core of his evolutionary system, consequently, we find a continuous effort to show that in the life and thought of Christianity, we have the only religious organism capable of giving full meaning to the universe which man has discovered. And this is precisely the criterion of its truth as a religion, namely that through revelation "the world as a whole takes on a maximum of coherence for our intelligence and a maximum of appeal to our taste for action." [11] His whole approach to the problem of God, his whole message to modern man was "to make manifest this coherence and to show how solid, natural and total it is." [12]

What Teilhard is attempting to do, then, is to give a basis for believing in the existence of God which could be discussed and established in function of both man's experience of modern life and his experience of Christian faith. The common denominator in each case is human aspiration. He says:

Let us look well, and we shall find that our faith in God, however isolated it may be, awakens in us a flood of human aspirations. It is in this original source of strength that we must immerse ourselves once more, if we really want to communicate with our brother men.[13]

In Teilhard's case such communication necessarily took place in the context of evolution, since he felt this to be the greatest single discovery of modern man about himself. He was convinced that the Christian phenomenon had to be seen within the evolving human phenomenon, and to help people to do so, believer and unbeliever alike, he elaborated a dialectic which sought first to show man's need of a transcendent God if evolution is to succeed, and then to show that only faith in Christ can fulfill that need. Let us consider now both poles of what Teilhard calls his "dialectic of spirit."

II

What brought Teilhard as a scientist and a philosopher face to face with the problem of God and the question of belief was his search for a successful outcome for the evolutionary process. His whole psychological preoccupation was, as is well known, with unity and synthesis, and his search for these in his personal life could not but find its counterpart in his life as a scientist. This is the ultimate reason that he searched in scientific data for some law which might allow him to trace the movement of evolution from its beginnings up to the present and thereby situate the human species within the total cosmic phenomenon. The law he elaborated, that of "complexity-consciousness," says that a higher degree of interior consciousness will always correspond in the experimental order to a higher degree of organic complexity. Since in the case of man we have the most complex of organisms, the human brain, we find here as a consequence the highest degree of consciousness, namely the power of reflection. Teilhard did indeed extrapolate this law into the past to explain the origin both of life and of thought, but his primary concern was to know what this law could tell him of the future. In essay after essay, as well as in *The Phenomenon of Man*, he repeats in different contexts and with different emphasis his central argument, and its brief outline here will show how it forces the reader to consider the necessity of an absolute.[14]

For clarity's sake we might divide what he says into three stages. The first is his insistence that man must be able to see some goal for his activity on earth, that is to say, some terminal point where organically he can develop no further in complexity or, as a consequence, in consciousness. For the movement of cosmogenesis continues in man and becomes a noogenesis in which the human species moves forward by the increasingly complex interplay of that which is specifically human, namely interpersonal relationships on the level of thought, freedom and love. It is precisely the sudden recognition by contemporary man that as a species he is incomplete and that his future development hinges upon his freedom, which has given rise in him to those feelings of anxiety and futility which characterize his life today.

In broad terms it may be affirmed that the Human, having become aware of its uncompleted state, cannot lend itself without reluctance, still less give itself with passion, to any course that may attract it unless there be some kind of discernible and definitive consummation to be looked for at the end, if only as a limit. Above all it rejects dispersal and dissolution and the circle from which there is no escape. . . . There must be some peak disclosed at the end of the journey, some transformation capable of giving life. Only such an outlook, only such a hope is ultimately capable, even

36

under the painful lash of material needs, of sustaining our forward progress to the end.[15]

This conviction of the necessity of man's having some ultimate goal for his action leads Teilhard to a second stage in which he rejects absolutely the possibility that this goal should involve total death. This accounts, in fact, for his many criticisms of Marxism.[16]

Those who think on Marxist lines believe that all that is necessary to polarize the human molecules is that they should look forward to an eventual state of collective reflection and sympathy at the culmination of anthropogenesis, from which all will benefit through participation; a vault of intermingled thoughts, as it were, a closed circuit of attachments in which the individual will achieve intellectual and affective wholeness to the extent that he is at one with the whole system.[17]

But such an outlook, Teilhard insists, is simply to work for the mere "well-being" of humanity, whereas what man in his heart wants is "more-being." This means that he wants to escape death, for ultimate death would mean that the world in which he lived and labored was hermetically closed and that what awaited the human species was the eventual triumph of entropy, pulling humanity back to the subhuman or to nothingness. The vast majority of men are not yet disturbed by this prospect. Today they still imagine, says Teilhard, that they can breathe freely inside an insurmountable barrier of death, provided they can think of it as sufficiently far away. But his own experience and that of many others indicate that tomorrow it will be otherwise. "A kind of panic claustrophobia is going to seize mankind at the mere idea that it could be hermetically sealed up in a closed universe." Why? "Because, . . . although reflective existence has always been oriented substantially toward survival forever, there can be no group experience of this primordial polarization until co-reflection around us has reached a certain important critical point." [18]

The "important critical point" in this text refers to that moment when the mass of humanity becomes aware of the importance of love for the unification of mankind. For without love, the only alternative for unification is brute force, exterior to man, impersonal, and in opposition to his need freely to choose his own future. But to have love we must suppose that evolution is a movement that does not destroy individual personality but nourishes it. This is why Teilhard insists that the process itself must be irreversible as far as man is concerned, and that death cannot mean the end of the person but must constitute a barrier through which there is passage to a new mode of personal existence. And because love dies in contact with the impersonal and anonymous,

A world culminating in the impersonal can bring us neither the warmth of attraction nor the hope of irreversibility (immortality), and without these, individual egotism will always have the last word. What is needed is a real *Ego* at the summit of the world to bring to fulfillment, without confusing them, all the elemental *egos* of earth.

Man's faith in the ultra-human, therefore, his urge toward *some thing* ahead cannot be fulfilled except by combining with another and still more fundamental aspiration urging him toward *some one*.

Only a genuine "super-love," the attractive power of a real "super-person," can of psychological necessity dominate, possess and synthesize the host of other earthly loves. Unless such a focus of convergence exists for the universe, not metaphorical or potential but real, no coherence is possible for totalized humanity and therefore no true stability.[19]

Let us note carefully at this point some of the implications of Teilhard's thought at the end of this second stage. Up to now what he has said is that man will never give himself to the work of building the earth unless he sees an ultimate goal before him and unless this goal somehow involves an escape from total death. But to be convinced of this he must likewise be convinced that the goal he is striving for must somehow be capable of nourishing personal love and therefore be itself personal, since love is the highest form of human energy and is alone capable of motivating truly human action. Teilhard quite candidly calls this analysis "an act of faith," by which he means not a religious act, but an option that the world in which we live is ultimately intelligible and does not involve absurdity. An act of faith in this sense, accounting for the totality of experience, is synonymous, he says, with "an intellectual synthesis" and calls for the intervention of a personal decision.[20] When such a decision takes place, then we have "the inevitable intrusion of the problem of God" into science and evolution.[21] Only by postulating the existence of God can we come to an understanding of evolution which is coherent, and coherence for Teilhard is, as we have already noted, the final criterion of truth. In evolution he saw not simply a scientific hypothesis, but an experimental affirmation of the coherence of being. By following out to the end all the implications of such coherence, Teilhard felt one had to speak of its ultimate source. "Once it is admitted," he wrote to a friend, "that being is better than its opposite, it is difficult to stop short of God; if it is not admitted, discussion ceases to be possible." [22]

We are in a position now, I think, better to understand the third stage of Teilhard's effort to show that the key which unlocks the meaning of evolution is man's need of an absolute. This third stage deals with what Teilhard insists must be the attributes of the God whom man can discover by following out all the implications of the evolutionary process. These attributes appear in *The Phenomenon of Man* but some of their presuppositions do not come through as clearly there as in other texts. There is, first of all, Teilhard's emphasis upon God as a person. In 1940 he wrote of the world war that "the root of the evil is not in the apparent conflicts, but very far from them, it seems to me, in the inner fact that men have despaired of God's personality." [23] By this he meant, of course, that man as a person will tend always to fail in love for other men insofar as he does not recognize a divine center for the universe who draws men to Himself and to each other precisely as persons, which is to say by love. Unless man accepts a personal God who loves him, all the accumulated potential in the individual, in a given society and in the world at large, will become oriented toward disorder and violence rather than to unification and love. This conviction explains his frequent appeals "that we should overcome the 'anti-personalist' complex which paralyzes us." [24] It also explains his opposition to the pantheism of Eastern thought, which did not distinguish between individual and person and whose ideal of union with God tended to do away with both.[25]

The second attribute which Teilhard stresses is God's actuality. Here again the center of attention is on the need for the success of evolution of Someone "loving and lovable *at this very moment.*" Love, Teilhard says:

> becomes impoverished with remoteness in space,—and still more, much more, with difference in time. For love to be possible there must be co-existence. . . . Neither an ideal center nor a potential center could possibly suffice. An actual and real noosphere means an actual and real center.[26]

In Teilhard's system, therefore, evolution is not in any sense an autonomous or spontaneous movement of growth in consciousness. It is due not to some mechanical thrust from below but to an attraction from above, "an inverse form of gravitation," as he calls it.[27] This attraction is that exercised by Someone loving upon someone loved, and the more individual men experience the reality of God's love in their lives, the more they themselves will be drawn to him and hence capable of contributing to the growth of spirit. "The spiritual value of a man . . . depends upon the degree of actuality which God has assumed for him; not the degree of speculative or even affective perfection, but, I repeat, the degree of actuality." [28]

Finally there is a third attribute of God which is stressed frequently, namely His transcendence. While it is legitimate to point out that in Teilhard's system the immanence of the divine action in evolution is so emphasized that the *sense* of its transcendence sometimes gets lost, it is nonetheless clear that the *concept* of transcendence is never absent from his thought. Indeed the transcendence of God is quite essential, since an actual personal center of evolution can in no sense be the product of such evolution. To satisfy the ultimate requirements of our action, says Teilhard, God "must be independent of the collapse of forces with which evolution is woven. . . . While being the last term of [evolution's] series, He is also *outside all series*." And in another text he says that "in short, God shows Himself to us as a *hyper*-center and also inevitably at the same time as an *auto*-center. He is, at least in His most essential self, transcendent, that is to say, independent of evolution, because He exists independent of time and space in that center which is Himself." [29] Evolution has, then, what Teilhard calls a "transcendent nucleus," or a "transcendent face," which lies behind that "immanent face" of which we spoke in describing the first stage of his dialectic. This "immanent face" is the terminal point of noogenesis, that collectivity of consciousness which man can discern at the end. What forces man to look behind this foreseeable summit of the evolutionary cone is the problem of death. For in order to guarantee that man's total development as a person in freedom, consciousness and love will not in the end disappear, there must be a face to evolution which man cannot see, and this must be a Person, actually attracting the human person by love, and bringing the movement of life on earth to a successful close on the other side of the death barrier.

We may bring to a close this treatment of the first pole of Teilhard's dialectic on the problem of God by noting briefly one corollary to this attribute of transcendence, namely our inability directly to experience God's activity in the universe. This follows, first of all, from the fact that the divine action is capable of simultaneously affecting the totality of the universe and all things in it, so that it can at the same time be present everywhere yet not be apprehended by any single individual. Secondly, this same divine action is capable of reaching the deepest part of man, the very center of his being, and of this center of himself man has no direct experience. "Thus," concludes Teilhard, "the precise point touched by the divine power is essentially extra-phenomenal, in the first case because of the degree of its extension, in the second because of the degree of its depth." And then he adds by way of summary:

"Properly speaking God does not make things, rather He makes things make themselves." [30] For Teilhard, then, God's activity always takes place under what he calls the phenomenal veil.

For Christian transformism, God's creative action is no longer seen as abruptly inserting its work into the midst of pre-existent beings, but rather as *causing to come to birth* in the depths of things the successive terminations of its activity. It is not on this account any less essential, any less universal, nor above all any less intimate to things.[31]

Man's experience of God's absence is consequently an experience of His transcendence, and the hiddenness of God, far from being an arbitrary decision not to show Himself, is really a manifestation of an otherness which is not too far *outside* to be a phenomenon, but too far *inside*.

III

Thus far we have considered that pole of Teilhard's dialectic on the problem of God which concerns man's need of an absolute. We have not as yet mentioned the word "Omega," but it will be easily seen how Teilhard can apply this term, the last letter of the Greek alphabet, both to the "immanent face" of evolution we have discussed, that goal of collective consciousness which man must see at the end of the process, and also to the "transcendent face," that divine Person responsible for beginning the process and bringing it to completion in Himself. Now the second pole of Teilhard's dialectic consists in searching for some confirmation of the existence of such a divine Omega, or more exactly for some indication that this transcendent Center of evolution has Himself spoken to man. "A presence is never silent," he once wrote. And in another text he says:

To admit, even by way of conjecture, the existence at the summit of the universe of an Omega Point, is *ipso facto* to introduce the possibility that some influences, some radiations of a psychic nature, circulate around us, betraying and at the same time confirming . . . the postulated existence beyond ourselves of an ultracosmic pole of personal energy. And it is here precisely that we

see clearly the meaning and importance of the Christian phenomenon.[32]

The second pole of Teilhard's dialectic will deal, then, with
that need of modern man which Teilhard sees as a concreti-
zation of his need of an absolute, namely his need of Christ.

What Teilhard seeks to do first is to show the remarkable
correspondence between the cosmic function of Omega, postulated by his analysis of evolution, and what Christian revelation
tells us of the cosmic role of Christ. Thus what he stresses primarily from this point of view is that relationship of Christ
to the cosmos which appears so clearly in St. Paul, St. John
and in Greek patristic thought. Through this optic the Incarnation becomes the visible manifestation of the union of
God with mankind and the material world. This is why Teilhard speaks so often of the "universal Christ" and the "cosmic
Christ." Here again, as in his earlier approach to the need of
Omega through the problem of death, he is grappling with a
problem which is his own: "Were the exigencies of my personal religion," he asked, "so exceptional and so new that no
traditional formula could satisfy them?" Such a formula, however, was at hand in traditional Christian teaching, although it
had not been in the forefront of the Christian conscience for
many centuries. When Teilhard discovered it he gave it his
own distinctive interpretation: "The universal Christ, such as
I personally understand Him, is a synthesis of Christ and the
universe. Not a new divinity, but rather the inevitable interpretation of the mystery which is the summation of Christianity:
the Incarnation." [33] This outlook is developed at some length in
the Epilogue to *The Phenomenon of Man*, and it will be worth
citing the key text at length:

As early as in St. Paul and St. John we read that to create, to fulfill
and to purify the world is, for God, to unify it by uniting it
organically to Himself. How does He unify it? By partially im-
mersing Himself in things, by becoming an "element," and then,
from this vantage point at the heart of the matter, assuming the
control and leadership of what we now call evolution. Christ, the
universal principle of vitalization because born as a man among
men, put Himself in a position (maintained ever since) to subdue,

to purify, to direct, and to superanimate the general ascent of consciousness into which He inserted Himself. By a perennial act of communion and sublimation, He aggregates to Himself the total psychism of the earth. And when He has gathered everything together and transformed everything, He will close in upon Himself and His conquests, thereby rejoining, in a final gesture, the divine focus He has never really left. Then as St. Paul tells us, *God shall be all in all.* This is indeed a superior form of "pantheism" without trace of the poison of adulteration or annihilation: the expectation of perfect unity, steeped in which each element will reach its consummation at the same time as the universe. The universe fulfilling itself in a synthesis of centers in perfect conformity with the laws of union. God, the Center of centers. In that final vision Christian dogma finds its culmination.[34]

Having underlined the correspondence between the *cosmic* function of Christ, as developed in one area of Christian theology, and the cosmic function of Omega, as developed in his own system of thought, Teilhard goes on to underline the *personal* role of Christ and the significance of the Christian doctrine of love within an evolutionary world-view. In such a world-view, it will be remembered, love is the key to survival. For evolution to succeed, there must be growth of a universal love in the noosphere. But where in man's present experience of a universal love can we find the beginnings of such a love? Nowhere, Teilhard insists, more than in the life of the contemporary Christian for whom creation has become meaningful in terms of evolution and for whom Christ is the source of love.

Such a believer sees the history of the world as a vast movement of cosmogenesis, in the course of which all the varied fibers of reality converge, without losing their identity, in a Christ at once personal and cosmic. The Christian who understands both what is essential to his faith and what is the spatiotemporal interrelatedness of nature, finds himself (I am speaking realistically not metaphorically) in the marvelous position of being able, in the midst of the most varied activities and in union with the whole of mankind, to achieve a unique experience of communion. . . . Thus we see that Christ (provided He is disclosed in the full realism of His Incarnation) is in every way comparable to the Omega Point which our theory made us anticipate, for He tends to produce exactly the spiritual totalization which we await.[35]

These two roles of Christ in traditional Christian teaching, the one cosmic, the other personal, the one seeing Him as Lord of all things created and source of their stability, the other as the channel of God's love and the source of its presence among men, were responsible for what Teilhard calls "an ultimate and final definition of the Omega Point." Omega is the Person of Christ who, through His Incarnation within history and His Parousia at its end, acts as a unifying focus for three centers, one inside the other, which reach a point at the top of the cone of time. The outside center is the natural summit of the humano-cosmic cone; within this is the supernatural summit of the humano-Christic cone; and the innermost center is the transcendent Being who through Christ has made Himself also immanent.[36] Teilhard was convinced, moreover, that the Omega postulated by reason and the Omega acknowledged through Christian faith would eventually react upon each other in the consciousness of mankind, and in the end be synthesized together. He saw the cosmic in this way giving greater significance to the Christic, and the Christic in turn "amorizing" the whole of the cosmic.

A truly inevitable and "implosive" encounter, this, and its probable effect will be soon after to weld together . . . the scientific and the spiritual around a Christ identified at last, two thousand years after the confession of Peter, . . . as the ultimate summit and the only God possible for an evolutionary movement finally recognized as convergent. This is what I see ahead and it is this for which I am waiting.[37]

What Teilhard is ultimately suggesting then, in his whole approach to the phenomenon of unbelief, is that modern man try to look upon the world and to see what he sees. This means, first of all, seeing man's existence within the new perspective of evolutionary change, a perspective demanding faith in survival after death as well as in a divine center of unification who must make this survival possible. But to share his vision means also to see a correspondence between this "faith in the world," as he often calls it, and another faith, not a result of rational analysis but a response to Christian revelation. This faith in the Person and cosmic role of Jesus of Nazareth completed Teilhard's faith in the world, and gave him a certainty of an outcome for evolution which his own extrapolations into the future could not give.

From the moment that we admit the reality of an answer coming from above, we move somehow into the order of certainty. But this takes place not by reason of a simple confrontation of subject and object, but from contact between two centers of consciousness: an act not so much of knowledge as of recognition, the whole complex interplay of two beings who freely open and give themselves to each other.[38]

At the beginning of this discussion we noted Teilhard's realization that his own experience of God, both as a man and as a Christian, had to be conceptualized in the context of modern man's determination to dedicate himself to human progress and to become master of the world in which he lives. He was likewise painfully aware that the vast majority of believers were not trying to do this at all, and that as a result their belief in God would eventually become irrelevant, if not for themselves at least for their children. He insisted:

There is only one way for believers to bring God to the men of our time, and that is to share their human ideal, and to search at their side for the God whom we already possess but who is present among us yet as if we did not recognize Him.[39]

This "presence" of God to modern man, a presence experienced more often than not as an absence, is for Teilhard a presence manifested in and through the events of man's life in the world. Only such an understanding of God, he felt, was capable of bridging the growing chasm between Christian faith and contemporary culture. His Christology was a further effort in this same direction: faith in the Incarnation is precisely a recognition that God has become so immanent in human life that the distinction between sacred and secular must henceforth be considered more rational than real. The Christian experience is simply that of taking part in God's plan, and this plan embraces the whole of the universe, the secular and the sacred, everything which is the work of man, everything which is the work of God. Teilhard concludes:

And thus in the end, above the rediscovered greatness of man, above the newly revealed greatness of humanity, not violating but preserving the integrity of science, the face of God reappears in our modern world.[40]

NOTES

1. Gabriel Vahanian, *No Other God* (New York: Braziller, 1966), p. 32.
2. *Constitution on the Church in the Modern World*, section 11.
3. *Le Goût de vivre*, 1950, in *L'activation de l'énergie* (Paris: Seuil, 1963), p. 248. Quotations from English translations of Teilhard's works published by Harper and Row, Publishers, are used by permission.
4. *Quelques réflexions sur la conversion du monde*, 1936, in *Science et Christ* (Paris: Seuil, 1965), p. 164.
5. *Le Coeur du problème*, 1949, in *L'Avenir de l'homme* (Paris: Seuil, 1959, p. 339). (Eng. trans., *The Future of Man* [New York: Harper and Row, 1964], p. 260.)
6. *Quelques réflexions sur la conversion du monde*, 1936, in *Science et Christ*, p. 160.
7. *Note pour servir à l'évangelisation des temps nouveaux*, 1919, in *Ecrits du temps de la guerre* (Paris: Grasset, 1965), p. 380.
8. *Mon univers*, p. 124, in *Science et Christ*, p. 66.
9. *Comment je crois*, 1934, pp. 1–2. An unpublished essay.
10. Letter of June 13, 1936, in *Lettres de voyage*, Paris: Grasset, 1956, p. 207. (Eng. trans., *Letters of a Traveller* [New York: Harper and Row, 1962], p. 226.)
11. *Introduction à la vie chrétienne*, 1944, p. 2. An unpublished essay.
12. *Mon univers*, 1924, in *Science et Christ*, p. 67.
13. *La Foi en l'homme*, 1947, in *L'Avenir de l'homme*, p. 243. (Eng. trans., p. 192.)
14. References to most of these essays will be found in the second chapter of Christopher F. Mooney, *Teilhard de Chardin and the Mystery of Christ* (New York: Harper and Row, 1966), pp. 34–66.
15. *Sur l'existence probable, en avant de nous, d'un "ultra-humain,"* 1950, in *L'Avenir de l'homme*, pp. 361–362. (Eng. trans., pp. 277–278.)
16. On Teilhard and Marxism, see Christopher F. Mooney, "Teil-

hard de Chardin and Modern Philosophy," *Social Research*, 34 (1967), pp. 79–84.

17. *Comment concevoir et espérer que se réalise sur terre l'unanimisation humaine?*, 1950, in *L'Avenir de l'homme*, p. 373. (Eng. trans., p. 286.)

18. *Barrière de la mort et co-réflexion*, 1955, in *L'activation de l'énergie*, pp. 425–426.

19. *Comment concevoir et espérer que se réalise sur terre l'unanimisation humaine?*, 1950, in *L'Avenir de l'homme*, pp. 373–374. (Eng. trans., pp. 286–287.)

20. "On the strictly psychological plane . . . I mean by 'faith' any adherence of our intelligence to a general view of the universe. . . . *To believe is to achieve an intellectual synthesis.*" *Comment je crois*, 1934, p. 2. An unpublished essay.

21. *La Formation de la noosphere*, 1947, in *L'Avenir de l'homme*, p. 228. (Eng. trans., p. 181.)

22. Letter of May 11, 1923, in *Lettres de voyage*, p. 31. (Eng. trans., pp. 70–71.)

23. Letter of October 18, 1940, in *Lettres de voyage*, p. 262. (Eng. trans., p. 269.)

24. See, for example, *Le Phénomène humain* (Paris: Seuil, 1955), p. 297. (Eng. trans., *The Phenomenon of Man* [New York: Harper and Row, 1959], p. 267.)

25. On the importance of Teilhard's distinction between individual and person in his own system, see Mooney, *Mystery*, pp. 46, 179–180.

26. *Le Phénomène humain*, pp. 299–300. (Eng. trans., p. 269.)

27. *Comment je vois*, 1948, p. 14. An unpublished essay.

28. Text cited by Claude Cuénot, *Teilhard de Chardin* (Baltimore: Helicon, 1965), p. 391.

29. *Le Phénomène humain*, 301. (Eng. trans., p. 270.) *Esquisse d'une dialectique de l'esprit*, in *L'activation de l'énergie*, p. 152.

30. *Note sur les modes de l'action dans l'univers*, 1920, p. 4. An unpublished essay.

31. *Le Paradoxe transformiste*, 1925, in *La Vision du passé* (Paris: Seuil, 1957), p. 142, note 1. (Eng. trans., *The Vision of the Past* [New York: Harper and Row, 1966], p. 102, note 1.)

32. *Comment je crois*, 1934, p. 16; *Comment je vois*, 1948, p. 15. Two unpublished essays.

33. *Comment je crois*, 1934, p. 22.

34. *Le Phénomène humain*, pp. 327–328. (Eng. trans., pp. 293–294.) A much more detailed analysis of Teilhard's theology of Christ's relationship to the universe will be found in Mooney, *Mystery*, pp. 67–87.

35. *L'Energie humaine*, 1937, in *L'Energie humaine*, p. 192.

36. *Esquisse d'une dialectique de l'esprit,* 1946, in *L'activation de l'énergie,* p. 156.
37. *Le Dieu de l'evolution,* 1953, pp. 5–6. An unpublished essay.
38. *Esquisse d'une dialectique de l'esprit,* 1946, in *L'Activation de l'énergie,* p. 155. In *Creative Union in Christ in the Thought of Teilhard de Chardin,* an unpublished doctoral dissertation recently defended at Fordham University, Donald P. Gray has analyzed with great insight the various modes by which Teilhard correlated his two faiths.
39. *Note pour servir a l'évangelisation des temps nouveaux,* 1919, in *Ecrits du temps de la guerre,* p. 367.
40. *La Place de l'homme dans l'univers,* 1942, in *La Vision du passé,* p. 324. (Eng. trans., p. 231.)

4

UNBELIEF AND THE SECULAR SPIRIT

Langdon B. Gilkey

Secularity is in the air today, even as it was in the autumn air of Rome when I was there at the last session of the Council. And as many rather wild-eyed theologians have recently pointed out, accurately and so uncomfortably, this is the air that theologians breathe along with everyone else. We cannot breathe our own "religious" air, and if we speak as if we do then what we say is unreal, to the man in the street as well as to our students and, when we finally admit it, to ourselves as well.

I am, therefore, going to speak about what I regard as the central issue for theology today, namely the relation of belief to this secular atmosphere, and therefore how we can theologize, both as Christians *and* as modern and so, secular men, and do this honestly. Let us note that this is a different, and I think more accurate, question than the usually phrased one which sees this as a problem in "communication," namely how do I, who understand and comprehend the traditional message, communicate this message in secular terms to others who are secular? This is to pretend that we clerics and theologians are not secular, that we feel and so understand the eternal message in its own inherent terms, while others who are somehow more profane do not—and we are seeking for modes of translation

50

from our language to theirs. I think the problem lies deeper than this because we all share this secularity and so find the traditional message as difficult for ourselves as it is for others. Churchmen and theologians live in the modern world as do others—else we really *are* lost! And their feelings, attitudes, standards and categories of thought are formed there too. We shall communicate to ourselves and to others more easily and fruitfully if we admit this, and start with them at this point, instead of trying to speak *at* them from some point outside the modern spirit—a position which in fact we do not and cannot hold.

My aim then is to talk about the possibility of belief, and so of theology, in the world of modern man. This will be a preliminary effort, both because of time and, more important, because I can by no means yet claim to *have* a secular theology. This is merely where I think we might start if we are to think through our faith.

We shall consider those four central attitudes towards existence which to me express the modern "feel" for reality, truth and value, and so which are characteristic of what we call the secular spirit. These are unthematized in most of us, modes of awareness, so to speak, and therefore probably unconscious. At this level they permeate and shape the consciousness of all of us who are active participants in our culture's life, and thus they determine the form of every creative product of our time, even theology, making that product contemporary, relevant, and, for some later observer, "of the twentieth century." For disciplined reflection these basic attitudes become fundamental categories or concepts, the intellectual presuppositions of our age we would call them, providing the framework of discourse for every relevant philosophy or theology and so determining it as characteristic of our epoch—much as the familiar categories of Hellenistic dualism formed the framework for every potent patristic theology, heretical or orthodox.

These attitudes or categories which together form the modern *Geist* are, I believe, the following: contingency, relativity, temporality, and freedom or autonomy. One finds these in positivism and most language philosophy; explicitly, and in one mood, in the naturalism of Dewey, Nagel and even Santayana; explicitly and in a different mood, in existentialism; and they are elaborated elegantly in a rationalistic, system-building way (which is *not* modern) by process thought. They do, I think, express the implicit faith or sense of reality of most non-reflective men. Together they evidence an attitude towards existence which confines reality, truth and value to the immediate, the experienced, the finite and relative factors around us, and that finds empty and meaningless any reference to a realm of transcendence.

In many ways, as we shall see, each of them challenges and even threatens traditional belief and traditional theology, and thus arises the spate of problems that beset current theology. Nevertheless, as we shall also try to show, these same attitudes contain latent within themselves certain disturbing and inescapable dilemmas, which point beyond the realm of the secular. Expressing as they do the structure of our human condition, as we moderns apprehend it, these secular categories of our existence raise questions in life to which faith, and its reflection theology, is, I believe, the only possible answer. We shall try to deal with the negative and positive relations to theology of each of the four categories.

I

Contingency has been a word long held sacred in the Catholic tradition. It is there the springboard from which one leaps into the purer air of being; contingency meaning here a dependence which points beyond itself for its own sufficient explanation. The presuppositions of this conception of contingency as requiring a sufficient explanation that is *not* contingent are, of course, legion and take us far back into the quite different worlds of Hellenism, of the Fathers and of medieval thought. The important point is that the modern sense of contingency—the sense we are trying to explicate—is precisely one that rejects these same presuppositions and so this pointing beyond itself. What is it?

This apprehension of finite reality, arising as an end result of seventeenth-century science, has since been extended and radicalized, especially through Darwin's influence, and now it dominates most of modern philosophy as perhaps its pivotal concept. In general we can say that this understanding of contingency is that concept which most directly restricts modern thought to the radically given, to the immediate and its traceable interrelations. For the modern sense of contingency essentially insists that the given is arbitrary and beyond it there lies nothing, no ground, no ultimate order, no explanation, no reasons. Finitude does not appear set within a wider order that explains and so tempers its arbitrariness—it just appears and that is all that can be said; existence and thought alike begin and end with the given. The modern sense of contingency is the ontological base for the radicality of modern empiricism.

This most basic apprehension is expressed in positivism's insistence that no meaningful discourse can move beyond the immediate, that which is verifiable; that the concepts of ground, reality, cause, explanation and reason simply have no intelligible application if one goes beyond the given and its interrelations— the assumption being that there is nothing more than the immediate to talk about. In naturalism the category of contingency is defined by Nagel as indicating that, while, to be sure, there are *causes* for events, there are no *reasons*—and the causes themselves having no reasons, things as a whole just "are," and their being has no explanation. Santayana expresses this sense of radical contingency with his usual poetry: "Matter is the invisible wind which, sweeping *for no reason at all* over the field of essences, raises some of them to a cloud of dust; and that whirlwind we call existence. . . . In a contingent world necessity is a conspiracy of accidents." [1] Again things merely "are," and for absolutely no reason.

Perhaps the strongest assertion appears in existentialism, for which contingency practically defines the meaning of the word "existence." Here one does not observe contingency from the outside as a phenomenon of "things"; one grasps it from within as the character of one's own existence. Our being is, says Heidegger, most fundamentally defined as "being there," and he does not mean "being there for this or that reason," but *just* "being there," being posited—for the essence of being there

53

is the experience of being thrown or cast into existence. Our existence is thrown, but there is no thrower and so no reason for the throw. Apparently for all its proximate orders traced by science, existence comes at modern man as if out of the dark, from no further reality, within no ultimate order and for no ultimate reason—it is brute fact, the absolutely given, the ultimate arbitrary, the merely posited: beyond what is given there is merely a void. This is what contingency means in our age, and it is *this* sense of existence as ultimately arbitrary that makes language which moves beyond the given, whether in speculative philosophy or theology, seem unreal, empty and irrational to modern man.

It is clear at a glance how different this concept is from what in comparison we might call the "half-hearted" contingency of the classical Thomistic tradition. There contingency is not that which has no reasons at all; rather it is merely the non-necessary, and it is assumed that the non-necessary still demands a sufficient reason. Contingency for Thomism is such that it implies in itself a movement of the mind beyond the contingent to that which provides the ground or reason that contingency cannot provide. I shall argue that in many respects this notion is a valid description of the way we men *feel* our existence as we live it. But we should recognize that this view of contingency makes no sense to modern *thought*, which defines the contingent as precisely the opposite, namely that which, as the absolutely and arbitrarily given, does not and cannot point beyond itself for an explanation. Thus in the modern situation to argue philosophically from contingency to a transcendent and so sufficient reason for contingency, is to appear irrational instead of rational, for the concept of contingency with which one begins the argument simply and essentially will not allow such a movement beyond the given. Perhaps the deepest philosophical difficulty for contemporary theology is this wall which the modern view of contingency has built around the given, restricting thought to the immediate and thus preventing any movement by implication beyond that wall to the transcendent. I take it that the demise of traditional forms of natural theology in recent Catholic thought reflects a consciousness of just this difficulty.

To the optimistic mind of the modern American intelligentsia, the radical contingency of our existence does not appear as a threat to life's meaning. Their confidence in the intelligence and the liberal motivations of educated, middle-class man is such that they are sure that out of contingency, scientific and moral intelligence can create such small meanings as to foster and preserve the good life. This same contingency can, however, be experienced in another, more European mood. Here the heavy hand of blind hate is felt more sharply, upsetting ruthlessly the frail meanings of men and even eroding inwardly their vaunted powers of intelligence and good will. Then, within the terms of the same modern vision of things, we are in the darker-hued existentialist world.

The differences between these two philosophies are immense, and make the major debate in present serious philosophy. But note that the ultimate vision is the same: man is set within a universe with neither a transcendent source nor an inherent or ultimate order; it is blind Nature or a meaningless Void, not hostile, to be sure, but empty of purpose, indifferent, faceless. Thus, the meaning, security and value of man's life cannot come from outside himself at all; they come from his own efforts within that range of contingency. Man may use his wider natural environment for his purposes as in Dewey, or he may shrink in alienation from it as with the existentialists— but he cannot relate inwardly to it by mind or heart, and he cannot depend on it. If the symbol of God represents a cosmic or trans-cosmic source of security, meaning and purpose to man's life, we can now see how it is that in our time men say God has died for us.

Modern man, however, not only reflects as a philosopher on contingency. He is also aware of it and feels it as a man. That inward reaction to contingency is felt as the anxiety about our security, an anxiety that permeates our secular culture, both inwardly in our attitudes and outwardly in our behavior, both in our fanaticism and in our despair. Modern experience has

55

blocked out all sense of dependence upon an ultimate order, and so modern reflection knows no meaning to the words transcendent source or ultimate ground. But modern man in his ordinary existence shows himself by no means content with this void at the base of things; he realizes the contingency not only of things around him, but of his own being—and so he searches for an answer to this insecurity of being, which, apparently, he cannot stand.

The effort to create an ultimate security amidst the welter of contingent things is one of the pervasive characteristics of the world's secular existence, economic, political and social. Our frantic struggles after an infinite amount of wealth, power or prestige; our tendency to absolutize whatever in life we make the central source of our security and meaning; our panic when these supports of our frail being are threatened—all this shows our dim awareness of the non-being of our contingency, and our corresponding search for something that transcends this level, something that is not threatened by non-being. These aspects of ordinary secular behavior cannot be understood, or dealt with, unless one assumes a dimension of ultimacy in which this unconditioned void appears as a basic threat, felt and acted upon—and to which some answer must be found if man is to accept his contingency with serenity and courage.

The life of modern man as contingent reflects the dimension of ultimacy of his being, even if his thought about contingency does not. This dimension of ultimacy is not God—for most men it is the void of an unconditioned insecurity and meaninglessness of which they are aware when they sense their own radical contingency and that of all their works. Nevertheless, this dimension establishes a range of experience and so of meaningful discourse within which theological language, as an explication of an experienced answer to these ultimate questions, can find meaning in a secular age. In examining the questions which our contingency raises, we now know what we are talking *about* when we begin to talk about God as creator and ground of our fragmentary being.

II

The second general characteristic or category of contemporary life, central to all we mean by the secular spirit, is that of relativity, or more accurately, relativism—since the former can connote a metaphysical principle that is by no means relative! This is a product, not so much of the cosmology of seventeenth-century science, as it is the result of the historical consciousness of the late eighteenth and nineteenth centuries, and of the biology that grew out of this. The resultant sense of the relativity of all things in the passage of time—of the forms of the cosmos itself, of natural life, of our own species, of political and social structures, of the most significant historical events, the noblest of ideas, the most sacred of scriptures, institutions or creeds—practically defines our era.

We are, for this modern view, pinioned within the flux of history, determined in large part by all that lies behind us, shaped by all that surrounds us, and to be replaced by what follows. Our deeds, our artistic creativity, even our thoughts are formed by the fundamental social and intellectual forces of our era, and so they are relative to their time and place. None of these things is absolute, eternal, or transcendent to the flux. Nowhere in observable history is there anything of ultimate authority, for all, being in part human, shares in the relativity of all things creaturely. Any historical event or creation is relevant and of immense significance to what surrounds it and shares its general contours; but by the same token, it becomes irrelevant to us—if, to be sure, interesting—as it moves away from us in space and time. Can the code of Hammurabi be promulgated in Washington, or even in Rome?

The bitter pill of relativity, or as we prefer to put it in theology, the "historicity" of man and of all things human, was accepted and unwillingly swallowed by Protestant scholars from Schleiermacher on. As completely unknown to the reformers as to the fathers at Trent, this idea has led to the total reconstruction of Protestant theology. With equal courage, and equal fear and trembling, many leaders of modern Catholicism have swallowed the same pill, and have battled manfully to remain "orthodox" within the flowing sea of historicity—I refer, of course, among others, to that valiant swimmer, Karl Rahner, and now to Leslie Dewart.

Again the effects on belief, and so on theology, have been devastating. Where are the ultimate events of revelation when all in history swims in the relativity of time; what is the Word of God amidst the welter and variety of historical words in Scripture; what is the mind of the Church in this manifold of changing historical minds, each rooted in and so directly relevant only to its own epoch? The divine bases for faith and so for authority in theology seem to have fled with this historicizing of everything historical, leaving us with the tatters of human authorities—a "Hebrew" understanding, an "apostolic" faith, a "patristic" mind, and a "reformation" attitude. Above all, as the language analysts say, where do you *get* this word "absolute," and what is its possible legitimate *use*? Is anything absolute in nature or history; what do you mean by these words referent to transcendence when all experience is of the relative?

The loss of absolutes in any way, shape or form has certainly been traumatic for faith and so for theological method, and the consequent loss of concrete meanings in our ordinary experience for such words as divine, transcendent, sacred and so on has made theological language extremely arduous, if not quite unreal. But, like contingency, a relativism that is *thought* is different from a relativism that is *felt* or experienced. The former leads intelligence confidently to confine reality to the immediate. The *feel* of relativity in existence, however, knows no such confinement. For that feeling an ultimate dimension opens up, qualified by negativity to be sure, but nevertheless ultimate and transcendent: a Void of unconditioned meaninglessness which threatens all the relative meanings that passing life may have achieved.

For once total relativity is vividly felt, ultimate questions crowd in upon us, questions about the meaning of the very relative life we now know is ours. What is the possible significance of what we do, of the families we bear, the works we create, the communities or institutions we may help to build, the civilization and values we may serve—if all is relative? Are these too merely here and then gone, of concern only to those whose projects they are—but for the rest of ultimate insignificance? And if so, what possible meaning can our lives have, which gain significance solely by their participation in what we now see also to be relative? Can the relative ever give meaning to the relative?

In these most secular of questions—raised by each commuter on the 8:10 train—we confront again an inescapable search for some ultimate meaning that threads through the relativities of historical existence. For this secular anxiety reveals, I believe, that our small meanings are not, so to speak, buoyant alone; they sink into the sea of relativity if left by themselves. They remain afloat as significant only if they participate in a wider context of meanings which is not relative. Once more in the midst of—and precisely because of—the secular relativity of our existence, a dimension of ultimacy has appeared—the inevitable search for that ultimate context, for an unconditioned grounding for the values that give worth and zest to our contingency. Christian belief is by no means the only answer that men of our age have found; secular existence is suffused with other answers, progressivist, Marxist, nationalistic and so on. But at least now we can understand to what range of ordinary experience our faith in and language about the providence of God relates, and how therefore in a secular age we can make intelligible to ourselves and to others the promises of His purposes in history.

III

Another major theme of the modern consciousness is that of temporality or transience, the becomingness or mortality of all the things there are. All is in time, and time being in all things, each has its appointed terminus. The Greeks of course realized this transience; but, as with the older view of contingency, they never thought of asserting it about reality as a *whole*. Just as to Aristotle and to Thomas contingency pointed beyond itself to a level of necessity and utter rationality, so transience and becoming pointed the Hellenic mind beyond itself to a ground that was eternal being. The meaning of the modern sense of temporality or becoming—as of contingency—is, on the contrary, precisely the opposite, namely that any dependence beyond itself on what is not transient is denied. All is becoming, all is mortal, all causes and all effects come and go, and nothing else is real. Death claims all creatures, and there is nothing else besides creatures.

No wonder the traditional category of being, combining as it does necessity, absoluteness, rationality and now eternity, has had rough going in recent times. Almost every potent aspect of the modern spirit—contingency, relativity, temporality and transience—moves in exactly the opposite direction. The result, as traditional forms of Thomism have yet to learn, is that now every form of logical argument that tries to point toward this concept seems not rational but precisely irrational. To agree with this older Thomism, one has, in fact, to accept this older world-view on faith, that is, one has to "believe" first if one is to regard this as philosophy and not as fantasy. Thus what was once a natural theology based in large measure on reason alone —as the classical world understood reason—becomes in our secular age the last, and not even the first, section of a theology founded on faith.

In any case, of almost all the concepts in the theological tradition that seem meaningless and unreal to the modern mind, the primary one is surely eternity. Where on earth, asks the modern, empirical man, except in the unreal, abstract realms of mathematics, logic and fantasy, does this concept find its base in experience? What lodgment has it in reality when all our experience, external and internal, knows only transience, the death of all that once had life? Do we experience eternity in time, except poetically—and how, if at all, could we experience it religiously from an *historical* revelation? On what basis, except a verbal promise in scripture, now rendered relative for all of us by scholarship, do we speak of an eternal life, or a life after death? Is not all talk of such things just comforting illusion, the product of fears and of hopes—and harmful besides, since it dulls the cold shock of the prospect of our own death, that final term towards which all authentic existence, existence decisively at grips with its own reality, points? Such are the searching questions facing current theology which the fact of universal transience poses for us—questions which in unreflective form each layman's gaze asks us, whenever we try stumblingly to speak to him of the Christian answer to his own death or the death of his loved ones.

There is, then, no direct experience of eternity for transient men, and so, characteristically, modern reflection finds this category meaningless. However, as in the other two cases, human awareness, feeling, and existential questioning fail to obey these methodological rules. For the question of eternity, of that which transcends passage and death, haunts the psyches of our age, shapes our behavior and our fears, and causes our frantic efforts to perpetuate ourselves and the things we love beyond the ravages of time.

The shunning of all signs of mortality is such an effort, feeble in effect but the potent source of the vast cosmetics industry. The effort to produce something that will last, whose significance is not for a moment but for all time, is another— feeble again, but still the cause of much scholarly production. The belief that at least our nation, civilization, or thread of history is a part of the eternal grain of things and will not die, is also irrational, to be sure, but the basis of much secular life and confidence as well as of most political fanaticism. All alike show that the question of ultimacy, a dimension of the sacred, appears within each facet of contingency, relativity and temporality. The categories of secularity themselves, in existence, explode the secular worldview, and raise in all of us pressing questions about that which transcends the secular.

Apparently man is more satisfied in his thought than in his existence with the naturalistic diagnosis. He cannot live securely or creatively solely within the terms of the radical contingency, relativity and temporality of his life. He can think about things that way, but he cannot *exist* in that philosophical abode he has built. For he always seeks after surrogate ultimates by which to live. He raises the question of eternity in his most secular of pursuits, even though he cannot answer this question within their terms. Again, the task of theology is to point out this dimension of ultimacy that appears in the midst of our temporality, to show how this dimension in man creates his very humanity amidst the briefness of his animal life, and how it establishes a realm of intelligible secular discourse within the terms of which theological language about God's eternity may become meaningful even in our age.

IV

The three faces of modern existence so far portrayed—contingency, relativity, and temporality—might seem grim indeed were it not for the fourth, which is the source of whatever optimism and courage the modern spirit possesses. Let us note in passing that no confidence or courage comes to modern man from his wider, cosmic environment where, as we have seen, all is blind, relative and transient. In this sense he is truly "on his own," an alien set within a context that is irrelevant to his own deepest purposes, and whatever hope and meaning he has comes to him from himself.

The fourth category of modern secularity is the assertion of the freedom and so the autonomy of man, of the inalienable and inescapable birthright of man to know his own truth, to decide his own existence, to create his own meanings, and to establish his own values. This view began, one might say, in the Renaissance and Reformation, but has become stronger, more precise and more inward since then. It increased in the Enlightenment drive for intellectual freedom, and in the Romantic movement's emphasis on the uniqueness and inwardness of individual feeling, and has been made fully explicit in our day in existentialism, psychoanalysis and democratic theory. As a concept, this category of freedom or of self-direction is both descriptive and normative. It is descriptive in the sense that it specifies the conditions in which man becomes fully man, the conditions of a true humanity; it is normative simply because these conditions are never reflected in the actual situation, individual or social.

In any case, this is the strongest voice of modernity, and the most creative. It lies in back of the important notions of scientific method and of scholarly integrity; and it is the deepest theoretical basis of our educational institutions, our creative political structures, our social reform, our burgeoning psychoanalysis and counseling; and it provides the deepest themes for our current literature and theology. If it believes anything at all, the modern spirit holds that a man must somehow live his own life in autonomy, making his own decisions and determining his own values; and thus any external authority can in the end only crush his humanity if his own freedom does not fully participate in whatever that authority represents. Nothing expresses this spirit more than do the writings of Karl Rahner, and many of the important documents of Vatican II. Ironically, this autonomy of man in freedom and self-direction is rigorously challenged if not denied by the *conclusions* of modern science, which tend to see man as a determined object, determined by genetic, neural, physiological and social forces which direct him and which he cannot direct—except when scientists talk of the *uses* of science, and then the sense of autonomy, freedom and moral choice becomes louder than ever before.

It is perhaps an over-assessment of the possibilities or capacities of this freedom that the two main traditions of modern philosophy diverge. The naturalistic, typically American, tradition, despite its metaphysical belief that matter is prior in causality, sees in a free, scientific intelligence and an emancipated democratic morality the possibility of the creation of meaningful structures in our natural and social relations; the existentialist, typically Continental, tradition, while giving freedom a firmer ontological base, still takes a dimmer view of these possibilities and views this freedom as only the more inward capacity of authenticity in the face of a meaningless cosmos and an equally erratic history.

It is obvious how subversive of traditional religion, with its authorities of various sorts, and of classical theology—with its requirements of faith, obedience, submission and self-surrender—this assertion of freedom and of autonomy has been. Is not revelation the denial of all autonomy in inquiry and rationality; is not a divine law the denial of personal autonomy in ethics; is not God, if he be at all, as Nietzsche said, the final challenge to my autonomy as a man? Religion, said Feuerbach, drains away all the vitality and interest man may summon for autonomous efforts; it smothers the infinite possibilities of control over his own destiny which man might exert; and it makes of him a submissive, weak, empty creature dependent on unreal forces beyond him. So the argument runs—and the history of the struggles against freedom by religious authorities hardly refutes this secular thesis, wielded so powerfully in our day by philosophers, psychoanalysts and social scientists alike!

What are we to say to this? Certainly, I believe, we must be humbly grateful to our secular critics over the years for their staunch defense of freedom and autonomy. For this should have been, had we but known it, part of our own witness as well—though most of us who have long overlooked this fact, now find this modern theme firmly emblazoned for all to see in scripture or patristics! The secular world, with its emphasis on freedom and on humanitarian concern, has been a more faithful and prophetic critic of the Church than she has been of her world, and much of what is now creative in our church life was stubbornly resisted when it was first chanted by the anti-religious voices of the past.

But we can, I also believe, point out how freedom, even secular freedom, does not lead to the autonomy or self-direction that is its goal. Man has come of age in the sense that now no traditional authority can without his participation determine his beliefs, impose on him his standards, or fashion for him the meaning of his life. He is on his own in history, and the Church will continue to be there only through his free participation in it, if it be there at all—which is as it was at the beginning.

Freedom is, however, our strangest and most wayward gift or burden. We are free of external authority in the modern age—*but* we are palpably not free either of Fate or of our own waywardness, and both are as much of a radical challenge to our real autonomy as they ever were.

The modern dream that by being free to think as he wished and to act as he willed—to be free of priests, kings, presbyters and the heavy hand of traditional authority—man could be free of destiny and construct life as he might dream or plan it, has been shown to be an illusion. We do not enjoy such control over our destinies: each effect of the free intelligence and will of man creates a new and seemingly unavoidable destiny for the moments that follow in time—as automation, the growth of weapons, the proliferation of cities, and the oneness of the world illustrate. Fate seems to ride into history on the back of human freedom as easily as it did on that of the ancient authorities. And the dream of a planned existence, where the free mind (of an elite, to be sure) has rationalized all of fate, merely bodes, to the sensitive spirit, a new and more deadly threat to the autonomy we cherish. Freedom and fate are not opposites, but always in dialectical relation—and the ultimate question of man's freedom over historical fate is as much with us as it ever was.

The second dream of modern, autonomous man was that a free man would be both rational and moral, and so free not only from authority but even more from his own sin. This too has evaporated with experience. We are still as weakly rational and as infrequently moral as our unfree predecessors; we too do the evil we would not—and especially when we exert our new power with the best intentions, as Vietnam illustrates. And the reason is that these good intentions by no means guard us from the hostility, the aggression, the cruelty and the selfish interests which we regard as sin in other men. Ironically also, each new realization of freedom in our domestic history, and in the colonial nations too, seems to unleash new and more terrible forms of the demonic in all of us, both in the oppressors and in the oppressed. A rational and moral control over our own freedom seems not to be there as a part of our autonomy, and no historical change can apparently create that possibility. We are bound within our freedom, doing the evil we abhor, fully as much as were the first-century readers of Paul's letter to Rome.

Incidentally, let me note as an aside that the evident bondage of man's freedom to sin is no basis for the imposition of a new authority, political or ecclesiastical, on that freedom. For as history well illustrates, the problem extends into the heart and actions of authority as well, and the more power we give to these the more desperate is our plight. God has granted much to his ecclesiastical servants, in both worldly and spiritual goods; but evidently one thing has not been given them in full measure, and that is any transcendence of this most human of problems, and hence any really trustworthy safeguard against their own misuse of their spiritual authority.

Again in the midst of our ordinary life, secular or Christian, arise ultimate questions which freedom in existence poses and which points us in our very use of our freedom to a level beyond it, to a level of ultimacy. These are questions of value, of that ultimate standard by which we guide our self-direction; questions of ultimate commitment, of that ultimate concern around which we are to center our lives; questions of guilt and so of an acceptance of ourselves which we can accept; and finally questions of reconciliation, of a power wherewith we may become whole again both within ourselves and with our fellows. Secular life tries in a multitude of ways to answer these questions, but without success, and the search for an ultimate image for our identity, for an inward forgiveness, self-acceptance and the power of reconciliation goes on apace throughout our secular existence.

In our freedom, as in the other facets of our existence, we touch a level of ultimacy which secularity did not expect. More than in any other area of our existence, nature here asks for grace: for the gift of an image of man by which to model our freedom, of a divine sovereignty to which to commit our freedom, of a divine love and forgiveness by which our wayward freedom may accept itself again, and of a reconciling power with which broken community can begin again. These are secular questions, in the heart if not on the lips of every secular man. Secular life knows their terrifying urgency even when it has no healing answers. In terms of these questions, a meaningful theology will understand the role of Jesus Christ, of the divine judgment and love through Him, and of the healing grace of God.

V

What is it we have been saying about secularity, belief, and the shape of the new theology? First, certainly that the secular spirit which envelops us all has forced the reconstruction of theology all along the line. For the way in which we apprehend our being in the world carries with it a vastly different set of presuppositions than was evidently true for our forebears. We live in a world in which all we meet and understand manifests itself as radically contingent, as relative and as transient, a world in which there appears neither an ultimate ground nor an order; and we understand ourselves as blessed and burdened with an inward freedom which we alone must actualize if we are to be men.

On one level this set of basic concepts appears to make belief impossible, theology irrational and empty, and religion irrelevant if not harmful. And this has been the diagnosis of our naturalistic, positivistic, and existentialist age, reflected in the recent radical theologies. Their diagnosis of our spirit, our self-understanding, the way we *look* at life, is, I believe, correct—but we have disputed their diagnosis of our real situation.

For on the level of secular *existence,* if not of thought, that situation reveals itself as one in which contingency, relativity, temporality and freedom continually raise questions which point to and so reflect a dimension of ultimacy in our existence which secularity cannot comprehend. In each phase of our being ultimate questions are posed. Of these we are dimly aware in our anxieties and our resultant frantic behavior; they appear in consciousness when we seek to make explicit our self-understanding and ask familiar and universal questions about our identity and destiny; they become the major themes of most of the literature that moves us; and they can finally become fully evident to a phenomenological analysis of human existence. This level of ultimacy is the region of our total experience within which our humanity reveals itself in its peculiar characteristics, and where the kind of language about ultimacy of which theological discourse is one example takes on meaning and relevance.

A theology that is on the one hand relevant and meaningful to secular experience, and on the other expressive of the answers of our classical tradition, will, I think, seek to understand the great Christian affirmations about God, as creator, ruler and redeemer, as answers to the secular questions of security, meaning, temporality, freedom and guilt. If we can write theology so that it comprehends its answers in terms of the problems of secular existence, and if we can in belief so face our ordinary life that it is illumined and redeemed by the answers of our faith, then both our faith and our existence in the world will be creative and meaningful for our time.

NOTE

1. George Santayana, *The Realm of Matter* (New York: Scribners, 1930), pp. 94, 99. (Italics added.)

THE UNBELIEF OF
THE CHRISTIAN

John Courtney Murray, S.J.

I SHOULD LIKE TO BEGIN with a somewhat general remark which is related to the theme of my discourse. There is one thing that has to be said about the massive phenomenon of contemporary unbelief, namely that the issue it presents to the Christian is not to be resolved by argument in the academy or by the academy. The issue can only be resolved in the order of action and history, by the whole people of God in dialogue and in cooperation with the whole people temporal. What we are confronted with today is not classical atheism, by which I mean a simple denial of the existence of God on the ground that the whole concept of God is unintelligible. The Marxist, for instance, is quite willing to admit that the notion of God is conceivable and even intelligible. The whole contemporary problem rather arises from the fact that atheism has now found a positive basis. It is now based on an affirmation, an affirmation of the human person, his dignity and his freedom. And this affirmation is accomplished by a will to achieve the dignity of the person by achieving his autonomy, by liberating him from the indignity and misery to which he is subjected throughout large areas of the world. There is today a new confidence that

John Courtney Murray, S.J., died on August 16, 1967.

man has within himself resources, purely human and secular resources, which are sufficient to organize the world in such wise that it will be a proper habitation for the man who is conscious of his dignity and freedom.

Therefore the Christian position today confronts a new counter-position. This counter-position is fairly simply stated. It says that there is only one history, the history that man makes and the history that makes man. The only forces operative in history, the only energies that galvanize history, are the energies immanent within man himself, his intelligence and his will, along with the modern prolongation of these energies which goes by the name of technology. And as for salvation, if there must be talk of salvation, the only form that man can hope for is a salvation to be achieved within history, by history, and by man himself, unaided.

Against this counter-position the Christian has to reaffirm the position that there are two histories. There is human secular history of which man is the agent, whose events are empirically observable and whose meaning is accessible to intelligence. But there is also, the Christian says, salvation history, whose operative principle is theandric, and whose basic agent is the Spirit of God. This Spirit, the Holy Spirit, is the power of God most high, who in this history summons men to be His co-workers, as Paul says in 1 Cor. 3:9 and Col. 4:11. The events of this sacred history are not empirically observable and their sense, that is to say, their direction, is not accessible to human intelligence but only to faith. These two histories the Christian says are distinct but not separate or separable. They are as it were two currents that flow through time together. They are coterminous in time. They began at the same moment and they run together, but they are not homogeneous in kind. One of them will end with the consummation of this world, the other is destined for a consummation beyond this world. Moreover, while the two histories run together, they are related in such wise (and this I think is the crucial point today) that the salvation of man even within the finite horizons of human history is mysteriously dependent upon another mode of salvation of which the theandric history is the bearer. In a word, if I

70

had to state the issue that confronts us today in its broadest terms, I think I would be inclined to say that it could be put in this question: Are there two histories or only one?

Now within this large issue of the theological intelligibility of contemporary unbelief there is a narrower issue, at once more immediate and more urgent. For the Christian cannot simply regard unbelief as a brute fact to be accepted, to be faced, then perhaps to be forgotten. No, this phenomenon demands to be understood in the light of faith, and the immediate theological question is whether or not it can be integrated into the Christian understanding of the Church in the world, that is to say, of the two histories in their relation. It is to this question that I now wish to address myself.

I shall state a basic theme, and I would hope that this basic theme, if elaborated in two different directions, might lead us toward an answer to our theological question. I am very aware that I must speak in a somewhat tentative fashion because we are confronted today with a new phenomenon on which only recently theological reflection has been bent. My basic theme is that the Church is the sacrament of Christ. This notion of the Church was in a sense a conciliar ideal at Vatican II rather than a theme consciously developed, but it has indeed become a post-conciliar theme. It was taken up rather importantly at the international meeting in Rome at the end of September, 1966, and was the subject of two major discourses, one by the Dominican theologian Edward Schillebeeckx, and the other by the Jesuit scholar, Juan Alfaro.

This theme of the Church as the sacrament of Christ has, of course, deep biblical roots in the Pauline epistles, in 1 Corinthians, Romans and especially in Colossians and Ephesians. The background of the idea is not, as many think, the medieval speculation on the nature of sacrament which led to the definition of the seven sacraments. The background is rather the biblical notion of *the* sacrament which is the "mystery" of Eph. 3:3-4, where the Greek word μυστήριον is translated by the Vulgate *sacramentum*. In the earlier Pauline epistles the accent was on the eschatological fulfillment of the mystery of Christ, the mystery of God. In the captivity epistles, Colossians and

Ephesians, the emphasis is upon the present, here and now, history of what Paul in Col. 2:2 calls the mystery of God, which is identically the mystery of Christ to which he refers in Col. 4:3 and Eph. 3:5. This mystery is simply the divine plan of salvation as it unrolls in history from the first coming of Christ to the Parousia. It is identical with the power and the action of God as operative for this salvation of man. Hidden from eternity in God the Father, this mystery was uttered in the eternal utterance of the Son and the eternal breathing of the Spirit. Here in time, although still hidden by the veils that conceal from man the face of God, it is nonetheless manifested in a sign, in a sacrament. It is revealed, as Paul says in Eph. 3:10, through the Church which is the manifestation of the manifold wisdom of God and the epiphany of the salvific plan of God. The Church, therefore, as visible and as historically active, is the sign and sacrament of Christ who is here and now with us in the Spirit according to His promise. The Church is the progressive realization of the divine plan of salvation for mankind, that reconciliation of all things of which Paul speaks in Col. 1:20, and that fulfillment of all things of which he speaks in Eph. 1:10.

Now I think it is important to realize, certainly for the sake of this discourse, that the Church about which we are speaking here is the concrete, living Church, which is, as Vatican II made quite clear in Chap. 7 of *Lumen gentium*,[1] an eschatological reality in which there is an indissoluble tension between the "even now" and the "not yet." Even now the Church is, and is one, and is holy, and yet the Church is not yet one and is not yet holy. The Church indeed has been sanctified, washed by the blood of Christ, sanctified by the immolation of Christ Himself on the Cross. But the sanctification of the Church still remains an historical process which is not yet fulfilled, because the Church, even now the one and holy, is still the pilgrim people of God, capable at any moment of those betrayals that the original people of God were guilty of after their rescue from Egypt. One must therefore distinguish two aspects of the Church, but not dichotomize them. One cannot divide the institutional Church from the people who make it up, or, in

72

more scholastic terms, one cannot divide the formal from the material elements in the Church. And in this living, concrete, historical totality, the Church is the sacrament, the sign of Christ. It is the realization and manifestation of the mystery of salvation which is even now being wrought out, though it has not yet been fully wrought out.

This, then, very briefly is my basic theme. I suggest that this theme is capable of development in two directions both of which are pertinent to our present inquiry. It is the second direction which is more directly pertinent to the unbelief of the Christian, but I should like to go through the first development first.

The first development leads to a sort of dialectical tension which was completely unresolved by Vatican II. The Church, as we have said, is the sign of salvation for all men, the new humanity inaugurated by Christ, the existential realization of the deepest meaning of human history. On the other hand, the Church is simply the little flock. From a numerical point of view it is almost insignificant in comparison with the vast mass of men who do not know and do not recognize either the Church or the Christ of which the Church is sign and sacrament. This gives rise to the question of the relationship between this little flock which is already gathered and the literally innumerable multitude of men who are still scattered. Is the relationship simply extrinsic, between those who are inside and those who are outside? Or is there possibly an intrinsic relationship? In asking this question, I think we come to the heart of the theological intelligibility of contemporary atheism.

Here is the point, I think, at which to refer to the biblical problematic, because *prima facie* it would seem that the biblical problematic is stated in terms of those who are inside and those who are outside. On the one hand, there is the people of God, there is the people that God Himself knew, in the biblical sense, that is to say, the people whom He loved and chose and the people who in return loved Him and chose Him and entered into a covenant relationship with Him. And there are, on the other hand, what Paul in 1 Thess. 4:5 calls the peoples who do not know God but reject Him and ignore Him, in the biblical sense of ignorance. They have chosen against Him and have thus become captive to what Paul calls in 2 Thess. 2:7 the mystery of iniquity, that counter-action in the world which opposes the salvific action of God. These other peoples are thus under the power and rule of the kingdom of darkness. In the biblical problematic, moreover, it seems evident that the ignorance of these peoples is somehow culpable. They have somehow chosen to stand outside the kingdom of light. We can see this in the Old Testament indictment of the idolater, which is pitiless and even scornful. We can see it even more clearly in the first chapter of Romans, where we find Paul's indictment of the pagan idolaters which ends with the words: "Therefore they are themselves without excuse." Their ignorance was not simply ignorance; it was an ignorance that was culpable. The same problematic appears in St. John, in his classic statement of the contrast between light and darkness. The light came into the darkness, he says, and there were those who "loved the darkness better than the light."

Now while this biblical problematic is perennially valid and must not be dissolved, it was in fact the product of a polemic, or at best, if you will, an apologetic. The prophetic indictment of idolatry in the Old Testament and the passage in Romans were directed exclusively to the people of God. Neither Paul nor the prophets were talking to the idolater. This polemic has had in fact a rather long historical life. It was installed in ecclesiastical literature certainly after the Constantinian settlement, and it has been maintained in papal literature right through Leo XIII up to Pius XII. Only at Vatican II did the inadequacy of this problematic begin to be appreciated and understood. Then the Church became more aware of herself as situated in the interior of history and not above it, as situated in the world and not apart from it. There was the consequent awareness that the relationship between the Church and the world, the relationship between the two histories, must be a dialogic relationship which implies a certain give and take. The proclamation of the Word of God today, as Paul VI made very clear in his encyclical *Ecclesiam suam*, must take the form of what he called the dialogue of salvation.

Consequently we now feel the need to enlarge the biblical problematic without destroying or discarding it. To do so we have to take very seriously a traditional doctrine that the order of grace is not coterminous with the visible, historical, empirical Church. The frontier between the kingdom of light and the kingdom of darkness does not coincide with the boundary, as it were, between the visible Church and something we call the world. On the contrary, the order of grace is pervasive through all humanity and the action of the Holy Spirit which supports sacred history is also somehow supportive of all human history including secular history. There is therefore a distinction to be made. The distinction is between the Church as the public manifestation of the mystery of Christ and the operative action of the grace of the Holy Spirit. The Church represents the fullness of Christian faith; the Church represents humanity in its consciously realized newness, and as such the Church is the sacrament, the sign, the manifestation of Christ. On the other hand, grace, and very notably the grace of faith, is somehow operative in all men, even in those we think of in terms of the biblical problematic as "those outside."

In consequence of this new conciliar awareness of the Church and of this newly realized distinction, a number of new theological themes have been cast up. There is the theme of the belief of the unbeliever, and the theme of the anonymous Christian. There is the theme of implicit faith, Christian faith that is implicit in all men of good will, in all men whose will is to the good, in all men who are animated by the spirit of love. There is the theme of the distinction between the manifest and the latent presence of the sacred in history. All these themes, all these theological theories, are pertinent to the issue of contemporary atheism because they serve to establish an intrinsic relationship between the Church and the world, between the two histories. These themes have, moreover, considerable theological fertility. They serve to enlarge and to deepen our notion of faith and to bring us back to a more biblical notion as over against the more intellectualized version of faith which was prominent in the scholastic tradition. These themes have besides a great pastoral significance insofar as they illustrate the necessity and possibility of dialogue; dialogue between the Church, which is the fullness of belief, and the world, in which there is indeed belief but a belief which has not come to a conscious conceptualization or even perhaps to an integrity of commitment.

Nevertheless, there is, I think, a danger today that these themes, especially the anonymous Christian idea, might lead to some dissolution of the biblical problematic. If you push these themes to their logical absurdity, you might be inclined to say that there are today no atheists, neither in foxholes nor anywhere else. You might be inclined to say that culpable unbelief is not a possibility, is not a viable option for man today, that there is no such thing really as conscious refusal or rejection of God. You might, if you pushed these themes to absurdity beyond the bounds of logic, be inclined to repeal the condemnation of Paul: "So that they themselves are without excuse in their idolatry." This we cannot afford to do, for the biblical problematic must stand.

Thus far I have been pursuing the first development of my basic theme of the Church as the sacrament of Christ, namely the dialectical tension between the institutional Church and those who have no visible relation to it. There is another line of development, however, one more directly pertinent to the unbelief of the Christian. A hint of it is to be found in Section 19 of the *Pastoral Constitution on the Church in the Modern World*, where there is a discussion of the forms and roots of contemporary atheism, and where explicit mention is made of the responsibility of Christians themselves for this massive contemporary phenomenon. Christians, the text says, "To the extent that they . . . are deficient in their religious, moral or social life, must be said to conceal rather than reveal the authentic face of God and religion," that is to say, the presence of God here and now.[2]

Likewise in Section 8 of the *Dogmatic Constitution on the Church* we read that the Church "faithfully reveals the mystery of its Lord to the world, but under shadows, until finally the manifestation will be complete in fullness of light." [3] Now these are very interesting statements and upon them hangs in

76

a sense a kind of conciliar tail. For in these texts there is explicit reference to the culpability of individuals in the Church. There was a great resistance among the conciliar Fathers against any notion that somehow or other guilt or sin or defect or deficiency could be predicated of the Church herself. There was great opposition to what finally got into the document on ecumenism, as to the fault of the Church. With regard to the document on religious freedom, I can testify here personally to great opposition on the part of the Fathers to any notion that the Church herself had been guilty of default, defect and sin against the proclamation of that Christian and human freedom which is inherent in the Gospel. It was I who finally devised the formulation in Section 12: "even though there were some people among the people of God who did not act up to the example of Christ in regard of Christian freedom." [4] That is the best we could get from the Fathers, and you have no idea what a strain it was to get this much into the documents, namely that somehow or other, here and there, now and again, one or another person in the history of the Church may not have lived up to the fullness of the Christian revelation.

I must say, with all due deference to the Fathers of the Council, that they were the victims of a defective ecclesiology, very Platonic in its implications, as if somehow the Church were some supernal entity hovering *above* history and not involved at all *in* history or in the people who make up the Church. They seem to have acquiesced too readily in some division between the formal and material components of the Church, between the Church as sacramental and institutional, and the Church as an historical and existential reality. They would have been well advised to return to a stream of patristic thought which as a matter of fact they themselves had found without fully knowing it. As you know, in Chapter 7 of the *Constitution on the Church* they picked up the great patristic theme of the eschatological character of the Church and as soon as you get into that you get into the tension that I spoke of a while ago between the "even now" and the "not yet." This tension is a vital tension—the "even now" and the "not yet" exist in unity and simultaneity in the concrete living reality of the Church that you and I belong to, the pilgrim Church making its way through history.[5]

If you take this theme of the eschatological character of the Church seriously, as we in the post-conciliar age can do, then I think you are obliged to admit not merely that individuals in the Church can be sinners and sinful, but that the Church herself at any and all given moments of her earthly pilgrimage can also be a sinning and a sinful Church, even though at the same time the Church remains the one and the holy Church. While it is true that the Church incurs guilt only through her members, it is nonetheless also true that the guilt her members incur can rightly be predicated of the Church herself. In other words, you could apply to the Church in an orthodox sense the famous Lutheran dictum with regard to the individual: *simul justus et peccator,* at once just and a sinner. And this seems to me implicit in the explicit conciliar acceptance of the Lutheran dictum that the Church must always be reformed. In Chapter 8 of the *Constitution* there is mention of the Church as at the same time holy and always to be purified;[6] and the Church is, as the text goes on to say, in continual quest both of conversion and also of renewal. This is what the Council said, and we in the post-conciliar period are allowed to take it seriously.

It is at this point that I come back to my theme, namely that there is a certain ambivalence to the Church as the sacrament and sign of Christ. On the one hand, the Church is the explicit and visible manifestation of God's plan in history, of the divine salvific action, of the abiding presence of Christ in His spirit. On the other hand, the intelligibility of this sign and sacrament is darkened by the shadows that conceal rather than reveal the authentic face of Christ who is the image of the Father.

The first shadow that falls on the face of the Church and obscures its intelligibility as the sacrament of Christ is the disunity of the Church herself. In John 17:21 the Lord said it was by the unity of His followers that men were to know that He had been sent by the Father. The disunity among His followers therefore is an obstacle to belief in Him. This disunity

78

blurs the message of the Church, confuses her mission and obscures the significance of herself as sacrament. Note that I am speaking of the disunity of the Church, because here again Vatican II dissolved an older problematic. It used to be that you had the one, holy, Roman, Catholic and apostolic Church over here, then rather lamentably you had a group of separated brethren over there. But this will no longer do. Obviously the Council here did not follow out its own thought. In the *Decree on Ecumenism*[7] the Council acknowledged that there are ecclesial realities outside the visible communion of the Roman Church. There is the reality of the Word, the reality of baptism, the reality of faith, to some extent the reality of the Lord's Supper. These realities are not merely realities that sanctify the individual as such; they are also ecclesial, that is to say, they contribute to create and build the Church. In their ecclesial realizations outside the Roman Church, these realities play a role in the history of salvation. It is not then simply a question of the true Church over here and those unfortunately divided from the Church over there. No, the Church herself is divided. She is not yet possessed of her full ecclesial reality; she is not yet the one and holy, although she is even now the one and holy. Here again we have the eschatological tension.

You will see, I think, that at this point I am once more touching the ecclesial dimensions of the unbelief of the Christian. The Church is sacrament of Christ, Christ is the sacrament of the Father. The Church is the sacrament of Christ in the concrete totality of her presence and action in history. On the other hand, the concrete reality of the Church in history obscures, dims, clouds the visibility and the intelligibility of the Church as sacrament and sign of the mystery of Christ. Christ is forever the *lumen gentium*, the light of the peoples. In the opening words of the *Constitution on the Church*:[8] "Upon Christ as the light of the peoples, the Church herself, who is to be the sign of Christ, casts shadows." And it is in this ecclesial sense that I think I would first speak of the unbelief of the Christian. It is the unbelief *in* the Church and the unbelief *of* the Church. The basic notion here is the notion of the Church as at once believing and unbelieving. It is the notion of the Church as at once realizing and signifying in history the divine plan, and in some sense being a negative realization of this plan and an obscuring of it. It is in such terms that I would in the first instance establish an intrinsic relationship between the Church, the world of belief, and those outside of it, the world of unbelief.

In some such terms I think one could reach a unified theological understanding both of the Church and of the world in their mutual relationship. There are of course the other factors mentioned by the Council itself: the faults of Christians, the neglect of education in the faith, misleading exposition of doctrine and defects of individuals in the Church. But you might raise this question: are there not also ecclesial defects, defects of the Church herself? Are not these related to defective structures in the Church, or to defective functioning of her institutions, whether these institutions be of divine law or of human institution? Do we not find defects in the organization of her prophetic ministry and its prolongation in theological education, defects in her pastoral mission, organized less in terms of love than perhaps simply in terms of efficiency? The *Constitution on the Liturgy*[9] notes defects even in the liturgical practice of the Church, in so far as the liturgy is a proclamation of the Gospel. The present funeral Mass, for example, is a complete misrepresentation of the fundamental Christian theology of death. Instead of proclaiming the ultimate meaning of death as the beginning of the fullness of life in Christ, what it proclaims is *dies irae* and all that kind of thing. This is somehow an ecclesial fault, for we cannot say it is the fault of the one who composed the Mass; we don't even know who he was. This liturgy is an instrument of the Church used kerygmatically to veil from the world the supreme message which the Church has to give to the world. Similarly the social practice as well as the social doctrine of the Church as such has as a matter of historical fact obscured her message of salvation. There is no need for me to develop this line of thought any further. The point is that the Church is a burden and a trial to the belief of the Christian as well as a help and a support to this belief.

The Church does indeed fulfill the great mandate of Matthew

28:18–20, her apostolic mission to teach. But the Church also forever falls short in fulfilling this mandate. The Church exists in the world as the sacrament of Christ, and does indeed reveal by her existence and her action the mystery of Christ; but she does this in a shadowed and darkened kind of way, *fideliter sed sub umbris,* as the Council says.[10] By her own unbelief the Church bears an intrinsic relationship to the unbelief of the world, as well as a responsibility for this unbelief, insofar as she herself, destined to be the sign and sacrament of the mystery of Christ, conceals instead of reveals the face of Christ. Yet the dialectic still holds: because the Church is the revelation of the mystery of Christ, she imposes upon the unbeliever a responsibility for his own unbelief. Thus we rejoin the biblical problematic: "So that they are inexcusable" who fail to recognize and acknowledge Christ in the sign of Christ. This biblical problematic is at root an affirmation both of the accessibility and the obscurity of faith. It is an assent to mystery, an assent that is given not on evidence but on the Word of God. Faith therefore contains within itself the seeds of its own imperfection; belief itself contains the seeds of unbelief.

In my opening remarks I underlined what I feel to be the central issue in the contemporary phenomenon of unbelief, namely whether there is something else in human life besides the history that makes man. For the Christian affirmation is that there is indeed another history, the history which God makes, and which takes place in and through the events of human history. This history of salvation can be seen only with the eyes of faith and its external manifestation is a sign, the sacrament which is the Church. Yet this instrument of Christ's revelation has, in cold historical fact, obscured His face and failed to proclaim His message. This the Church has done not through malice but simply because she is human. Her members are therefore themselves in some sense unbelievers, and must share responsibility for the unbelief of the world around them. This world in turn cannot be absolved from its own guilt, for there will always be men who freely choose to live in darkness rather than in light. Yet what the Christian must guard against, when he and his Church present themselves to the world in which they live, is that this world should not encounter in them that portion of darkness which is theirs. This we all pray for, that the light which is Christ may break through our darkness, and that contemporary unbelief may find in the Church a sacrament of Christian faith.

NOTES

1. *The Documents of Vatican II*, Ed. Walter M. Abbott, S.J. (New York: Herder & Herder and Association Press, 1966), pp. 20–22.
2. *Documents of Vatican II*, p. 217.
3. Cf. *Documents of Vatican II*, p. 24. The translation here given is Fr. Murray's own.
4. Cf. *Documents of Vatican II*, p. 692. The sentence above appears in somewhat different fashion in this translation: "In the life of the People of God as it has made its pilgrim way through the vicissitudes of human history, there have at times appeared ways of acting which were less in accord with the spirit of the gospel and even opposed to it." In the Preface to *Documents of Vatican II*, p. xi, the following significant statement is found: "Although these translations are to a major extent my own [Very Rev. Msgr. Joseph Gallagher], there is one exception. . . . The translation of the Declaration on Religious Freedom was chiefly prepared by one of the architects of the Latin original, Father John Courtney Murray, S.J. For this volume, he slightly emended the translation he had prepared for the National Catholic Welfare Conference." In footnote 51 to the above version in *Documents of Vatican II*, p. 692, Fr. Murray wrote as follows: "The historical consciousness of the Council required that it be loyal to the truth of history. Hence the Declaration makes the humble avowal that the People of God have not always walked in the way of Christ and the apostles. At times they have followed ways that were at variance with the spirit of the gospel and even contrary to it. The avowal is made briefly and without details. But the intention was to confess, in a penitent spirit, not only that Christian churchmen and princes have appealed to the coercive instruments of power in the supposed interests of the faith, but also that the Church herself has countenanced institutions which made a similar appeal. Whatever be the nice historical judgment on these institutions in their own context of history, they are not to be justified, much less are they ever or in any way to be reinstated. The Declaration is a final renouncement and repudiation by the

82

THE UNBELIEF OF THE CHRISTIAN

Church of all means and measures of coercion in matters religious."

5. *Documents of Vatican II*, pp. 20–22 and n. 17.
6. *Ibid.*, pp. 22–24.
7. *Documents of Vatican II*, pp. 341–66.
8. *Documents of Vatican II*, pp. 14–24.
9. *Documents of Vatican II*, § III. Reform of the Liturgy, pp. 146–52 and *passim*.
10. Cf. *Documents of Vatican II*, Decree on Ecumenism, 6, p. 350.

PART TWO

THE CONTEMPORARY PROBLEM OF GOD

METAPHYSICS AND
THE CONCEPT OF GOD

Leslie Dewart

THE HISTORY OF RELIGIOUS THOUGHT shows two distinct ages in the development of the concept of God. Primitive religions conceive the divine as a reality which, as such, is of the same order as every other which falls under man's experience. God may have, of course, greater perfection—perhaps even infinitely greater perfection—than every other reality. But although God may differ from every other being in every other way, He does not differ from any other being precisely as being. He is, therefore, a being among other beings, a being in basically the same sense as every other being. Together with the sum of other beings He makes up the universe, the totality of being.

However, in the course of its development, human thought adverted to the inadequacies of every worldview which centers on what might be called a *physical* concept of God. Apart from the possible claims of Far Eastern thought, in the West at least it was the privilege of Greece to live through that stellar moment in the history of mankind when the *metaphysical* concept of God emerged. By this I mean the enriched concept of God as a reality which, precisely as being, transcended the order of being of which we had common experience and of which we ourselves formed a part. This transformation of the concept of God was made possible by a corresponding expansion of the concept of being. Over and above the being of the empirical world there was another whole order of being which differed from our world precisely as being. God was, therefore, not *the* Supreme Being: He was not the highest and first among the totality of beings who made up the universe. He was indeed Supreme Being—but His supremacy was of the order of being. He was supreme not primarily in relation to other beings: it was His being that was supreme.

It follows that in metaphysical thought "being" does not mean exactly the same thing when it is predicated of God as when it is predicated of other beings. However, it is equally clear that the term must mean somewhat the same thing, otherwise it would mean nothing intelligible when applied to God. The question whether this procedure is valid is most important. Once granted that there *are* degrees of being, the doctrine of analogy is the only explanation which accounts for our knowledge of transcendent being on the basis of our immediate experience of empirical being alone: if God is Subsistent Being Itself, there can be little doubt that being is predicated of Him and of empirically given being only proportionally. But does not the concept of God as Subsistent Being Itself presuppose the analogy of being? If so, we are involved in a vicious circle, unless perhaps the analogicity of the metaphysical concept of being were empirically grounded, derived exclusively from our understanding of empirically given being. It is a tribute to the perspicacity of Jacques Maritain that he was the first among the neo-Thomists to have realized that this was an implicit requirement of metaphysics, and hence the first to have asserted that there is a metaphysical "intuition of being," that the experience of being reveals being immediately and empirically as "intrinsically polyvalent," that is, as analogical. But the difficulty with this doctrine is exactly the same as that of the earlier doctrine of analogy, namely, that its undoubted apologetic advantages fail to be supported by empirically grounded evidence. In the last analysis, Maritain's doctrine of analogy simply reiterates the traditional gratuitous assertion that there are degrees of being. Moreover, if being could be experienced by the human intellect as intrinsically analogical, the existence of God would be quite as self-evident as that of created beings, God would be empirically given (at least to metaphysicians) in precisely the same way as any other being. We shall have occasion below, in connection with the question of the validity of metaphysics, to recall these difficulties of the doctrine of analogy. What is relevant at present is that metaphysical thought can be defined with reference to the doctrine of the analogical degrees of being. For this is the foundation of the metaphysical concept of God.

Two key problems arise from the tacit or explicit assumption of this metaphysical concept of being: what is the relation among the degrees of being, and how can we pass from the knowledge of empirically given being to the knowledge of being which is not empirically given. The exploration of these two problems spins the thread that runs throughout the history of metaphysics. Now, the progress made by philosophical speculation as it occupied itself with these questions can scarcely be minimized. Man's attempt to understand his religious experience probably made much greater gains between Plato and St. Thomas than in the previous five-thousand years of human culture. Nevertheless, these advances were made within the parameters of metaphysics; they mark the progress made within the confines of the doctrine of the degrees of being. (This is why, despite the historical multiplicity of specifically variable metaphysical doctrines, it is proper to speak in the singular of *the* metaphysical concept of God.)

But, within the history of philosophy, metaphysics eventually surpassed the order of inward transformation and in due course evolved beyond itself: the accomplishment of metaphysical thought is indeed in no way more evident than in its having transcended itself. It is a matter of historical fact that philosophy has entered a post-metaphysical stage—or, perhaps more accurately, it is now concluding the first stage of a new age which liquidates both its physical and metaphysical phases. Of course, many philosophers who, chronologically speaking, must be called contemporary, insist that metaphysics is eternally valid, and that the contrary suggestion reveals nothing but the regressive, possibly perverse, character of modern thought. In deference to them I will, therefore, make my assertion hypothetical: to the degree that the critique of metaphysics is valid, philosophical thinking about God must correspondingly take place in a post-metaphysical context. Conversely, a metaphysical concept of God is possible today only insofar as it is supposed that metaphysics has survived. But this is possible only if the logic of the history of philosophy is denied, and if a return to pre-Kantian thought is deemed imperative. Otherwise the question arises: how does the critique of metaphysics affect the philosophical concept of God? This is the topic I now propose to discuss.

I

The beginning of the latest stage of philosophical development was characterized, not surprisingly, by the rejection of the past. With Kant metaphysics reached the paradoxical conclusion that metaphysics was invalid. Indeed, the paradox was double, for metaphysics reached the conclusion that metaphysics was invalid, but nevertheless unavoidable. But this negativity and this self-contradiction point to the imperfection, not to the total falsity, of Kant's critique of metaphysics. With the advantage of longer hindsight we can now begin to understand that Kant's achievement was not the liberation of reason from the burden of an inveterate fallacy, but the disclosure of the possibility that it might reach new heights. The lesson to be learned from him is not that metaphysical thought, which ought never to have been born, should at least mercifully annihilate itself, but that metaphysics, which is the seed of later thought, can transcend itself if reason continues to develop itself. To enter a post-metaphysical age in philosophy (I suppose it should, in all purity, be called a meta-metaphysical age) is not, as Heidegger appears to think, to return to a forgotten truth: it is to pass through the truth of metaphysics into a philosophical truth beyond metaphysical thought.

The impact that the critique of metaphysics has historically had on the metaphysical concept of God is well known. But if the meta-metaphysical stage of philosophy is, as suggested above, the result of neither the valid nor the invalid rejection of metaphysics, but the outcome of the creative evolution of metaphysics, we would be ill-advised to suppose either of two things: that the metaphysical concept of God was the ir-reformable, final philosophical truth about God, which must now be recovered and preserved, or else that it was the basic philosophical mistake about man, an error which must now be exorcised once and for all. If we recognize that philosophical thought truly and creatively develops, the present period in the history of philosophy may be envisaged as a transitional zone (which we entered about a century and a half ago) beyond which may well lie a new level of progress in the history of religious thought. For the impasse of theism and atheism makes a great deal of historical sense, and must be envisaged as broadening the horizon of philosophical speculation about God. What justifies this hopeful estimate?

Modern atheistic thought is built upon the premise that metaphysical knowledge is a delusion. If the concept of being may not be extended beyond that order of reality which is open to everyday, common empirical understanding, belief in God is unreasonable and must be explained away in terms of empirically accessible realities—for instance, socio-economic forces, abnormal psychological mechanisms, or the projective nature of human consciousness. Now, modern theistic thought (at least in its Catholic variety, with which I shall be solely concerned here) holds, of course, opposite views concerning the reality of God. But not infrequently the extremes meet. Modern Catholic theism grants the formal validity of the atheistic conclusion drawn from the critique of metaphysics, and opposes atheism not as an unwarranted development of valid premises provided by the genuine progress achieved in philosophy in post-medieval times, but as the logically valid consequence of an original miscarriage of philosophy which it traces at least as far back as Descartes. In other words, theism has taken its stand on the validity of metaphysics, on the apparent assumption that the metaphysical concept of God cannot be improved upon. This means: Catholic theism is in agreement with modern atheism in one crucial respect, namely, in the supposition that if any concept of God is philosophically valid, it must be the

91

metaphysical concept of God. Conversely, because its response to atheism has been reactionary, Catholic philosophy has willy-nilly wed itself to the metaphysical concept of God. For the logic of its position has compelled it to cut itself off from modern thought, persuading itself that after St. Thomas a tragic and well-nigh total perversion of philosophy has taken place.

This reaction to atheism has been not only humanly understandable: it has had the merit of upholding important truths. For all its valuable criticism of the metaphysical concept of God, atheism suffers, in my estimation, from the definitive mistake of explaining away religious belief. Catholic theistic thought has been guilty of reaction, but it has cleaved to the fundamental facts of religious phenomena. But perhaps now it is time to do better than this, and to explore new hypotheses. If we recognize not only that the theistic tradition has retained, albeit imperfectly, what is valid in religious experience, but also that the mainstream of philosophy has, for all its inadequacies, run logically and creatively, the possibility that naturally suggests itself is that a *meta-metaphysical* concept of God might be developed. For it should be possible to understand philosophically that which physically and metaphysically has been traditionally called God, while avoiding, on the one hand, the pre-critical inadequacies of the doctrine of the degrees of being and, on the other, the unwarranted reduction of reality to that which is given in the immediate experience of being. This is the question with which I am concerned in this paper. But, in the first place, I must explain what the question means.

Given the conditions under which the question has been raised, the direction of the investigation is defined by two points. First: the reality to which the religious experience relates must be empirically accessible; that is, it must be, if not actually given in experience, at least revealed in the experience of that which is given in experience; it must be somehow signified empirically. To accept this is no more than to accept the general validity of the critique of metaphysical knowledge. (From this also follows a methodological conclusion: the nature of reality to which religious experience is relative is to be ascertained through an analysis of religious experience.) Second: if the critique of metaphysics is valid, a transcendent being is a contradiction in terms and, therefore, metaphysical theism is invalid. But this does not imply that the reality to which religious experience relates is not a transcendent reality, if the common assumption of atheism and metaphysical theism—that there is no empirical reality other than being—is questioned. For the reality which answers to religious experience may be transcendent, even if it is not being. In other words, the possibility to be explored is that the reality of God may be transcendent precisely because it transcends being. If we put together these two points, then the meaning of the question begins to emerge. The problem really is: whether the analysis of religious experience reveals a reality which transcends being.

In this formula the stress falls on whether the reality in question is or is not to be conceived as transcending being. Our problem is to be distinguished from the question whether religious experience reveals an "objective" or a "subjective" reality and, if "objective," whether this objective reality is best conceived in terms of "being" or otherwise. For the latter formulation would effectively limit theism to its metaphysical (or else to its "physical") form. A "subjective" God would be, of course, no God at all. But if an "objective" God were said to be a reality which transcended being, this might be taken to mean that the term "being" referred only to some objective realities, while another term (for instance, "reality") should be devised to refer to the transcendent reality of God. This would amount to a surreptitious re-introduction of meta-physical thought under the disguise of a novel but equivocal terminology, in which the "analogy of reality" would perform the same function that the "analogy of being" has in the past.

If we are to conceive God in a meta-metaphysical way, the question about God must imply a radical reformulation. A dilemma is implicit in the question "whether God exists," or in any variation thereof. The implication is that, in either event, God is to be conceived as being, as that-which-exists. For it is only of a God so conceived that we can say either that His reality is that of an objectively existing being, or else that it has no other reality than that which man can give it (for instance, as a projection of objective realities which pertain to the order of human existence alone).

Yet, the assumption that God is to be conceived as being is not unquestionable. A first indication of this is the invalidity of the ontological argument in all its forms. If God is being, then (unless He were a "physical" being) He must be Being Itself. But there is a contradiction between assuming that God is Being Itself and yet asking whether He exists, unless we admit that the concept of God as Being Itself is strictly *a priori*. Conversely, there is an *a priori* concept of God introduced into every argument which assumes that God, if He exists, exists necessarily. In other words, the critique of metaphysics invalidates not only the conclusion, but also the major premise of the ontological arguments. For these arguments involve a God so defined that He can never be related to existence. The critique of metaphysics shows not only that we cannot derive the existence of God from His definition, but also that we cannot define Him in relation to existence (except strictly *a priori*). Thus, the concept of God as being is an assumption which critical thought must treat accordingly. This means: if we first conceive God and thereafter ask whether He exists, we have accepted the dilemma, for the concept of God in relation to which the question is put must be the concept of "some sort" of being—since it is a concept of a God the reality of whom is, *ex hypothesi*, first conceived in the experience of (created) being and afterwards modified by negation and supereminence. To ask whether there exists a being who is transcendent insofar as He transcends our experience is to proceed backwards: what we must enquire is whether experience reveals a reality which does *not* transcend human experience, but which *does* transcend being. In other words, it may be that the "mysterious" quality of God, that quality which requires all cognition of Him to take the form of faith, is not attributable to deficiencies in either the nature or condition of our cognitive apparatus, but to the nature of God Himself.

This brings us to the root of the inadequacy of the metaphysical concept of God, namely, that it is essentially, and not merely historically, related to the physical concept of God. For we must remember this: the distinctiveness of metaphysical thought is not that it conceives God as being, but that it conceives being as analogical (and hence God as Being Itself). The concept of God as being originates with antemetaphysical thought, and a metaphysical God is simply a physical God from which all limitations have been removed apophatically, a God who is being in basically the same way as empirically given being (that is, by existing), but who is nevertheless *said* to be different from empirically given being precisely as being. Thus, the question "whether God exists or not" is made fundamentally possible by the assumption of an essential aspect of the *physical* concept of God, namely, that God is being, that God is (at least in part) like empirically given being, that the concept of being means "somewhat the same thing" when applied to God and when applied to man. This concept of God is thereafter complemented with negation and supereminence, as required by the progressive discovery of its deficiencies and contradictions. Hence, metaphysics conceives God not only as being, but as being *a se* and as Subsistent Being Itself.

In other words metaphysics is essentially relative to "physics." This is not an objection, but it is, if correct, an observation relevant to philosophical enquiry. When we today raise the question of God, our investigation is historically continuous, not only with classical Greek and biblical Hebrew thought, but with primitive Greek and primitive Hebrew thought—and indeed with the religious thought of mankind since earliest times. A re-formulation of the problem of God which sprang from an adequate critique of metaphysics would have to reject also the pre-metaphysical assumption of metaphysics, namely, that God is being or else nothing at all. It is illegitimate to ask "whether God exists" (or "whether there is an objective, and not merely a subjective, reality which corresponds to our religious experience"), because we cannot reasonably assume that religious experience is adequately conceptualized *a priori*, that is, in terms of a God who may or may not exist (or of a reality which may be either objective or subjective). The question of God must be so put as to allow the possibility of conceiving God *a posteriori*. Therefore, as I have formulated it above, the question means: what does religious experience reveal? What is the reality which at different times has been conceived physically and metaphysically as God? And is this not better conceived as transcending being than as transcendent being? I need hardly stress that on the present occasion only the most preliminary exploration of this problem is being undertaken.

II

The heart of religious experience—by which I mean simply experience insofar as it is the origin of religious belief—is the experience that being *as such*, that is, being in its existential import, is a matter of *fact*. For the most fundamental quality of conscious experience is that it reveals being to itself, and itself to itself, as being *already there*: it reveals being as something which is unquestionably a fact. The *cogito* shows this with great clarity: it is a fact that I exist, that things exist, that there is existence. What exists is *already* in existence, and it is never found except as being already there. For instance, man has to contend with the facts because the indeterminacy of the future begins with the factuality of the past. That which exists has been, as it were, already decided about—not in every way, of course, but precisely as existing. Therefore, any further decisions in relation to it must begin with existence precisely as a fact. Freedom and creativity imply that man's future is grounded upon his present self-apprehension in relation to his past.

Note, however, that the factuality of being is ambivalent. So far I have stressed only that a fact is indisputable, that it is what it is irrespective of anyone's wishes or imagination, and that therefore it is that which rules every human attempt to find meaning. On the other hand, this also implies that a fact is meaningless in itself. As the common expression has it, the facts are "only the facts," and it is not in vain that we frequently refer to the "bare facts." A fact is "nothing but a fact": it may call for interpretation, but does not of itself constitute its own interpretation. Its meaning is not set once for all by simply existing. And it matters little whether only one interpretation can be true, or whether alternative interpretations can be related within the catholicity of truth: in either event the facts as such are "only facts." Thus, if something is said to happen "as a matter of fact," we imply that we need not search behind it for a cause or explanation why it *had* to happen. The point is that although it *did* happen, it did *not* have to happen. Every explanation of what happens is *posterior* to the event. For explanations must fit the facts, not the other way about. The facts as such stand by themselves, without explanation or justification: they are that for which explanation and justification are sought.

The factuality of being should not be confused with *contingency* in the traditional sense of this term: it does not mean that being derives its indisputability from a *raison d'être* which, since it does not possess from itself, it must receive from another and, ultimately, from a being which is not contingent, but *a se*. If we were to observe, as for instance St. Thomas does, simply the paucity of self-explanation which accompanies factual existence, neglecting the obtrusive, self-assertive quality of whatever is a fact, then we would conceive empirically given being as contingent, in the simple sense that *it need not be*. But, if the contingent is simply that which need not be, then we would also have to say, as St. Thomas does, that "nothing is so contingent that it does not possess some necessity in itself." [1] This is an *a priori* concept of contingency, which understands contingency in strict relation to necessity. This conception of the contingency of empirically given being as the absence of necessity *presupposes* an absolute necessity in relation to which being exists and is a relative necessity. We may, of course, retain the term contingency (and I shall continue to use it here), provided we do not also retain its relativity to "necessity." If we wish to avoid the *a priori* assumption of an absolute necessity and yet retain the term "contingency," we must stress that it means *absolute contingency*. As empirically given, existence is merely a fact—but it is indeed indisputably a fact. On empirical grounds we are entitled to assert that being is, even if it only *happens* to be. It is inadequate simply to assert that it *need not* be—though evidently it is the fact that it is only a fact that permits us to say that it need not be. But every assertion that it need not be must be complemented with the assertion that nevertheless it is. Perhaps it might never have come into being—but now it *has* come into being. It already is, and nothing can be done to alter this. Even if it were to be annihilated, its disappearance would not in the slightest diminish (on the contrary, it would confirm) the fact that once it *had* been.

Hence, the point of affirming the contingency of being is quite the opposite of what metaphysicians have thought, and in this respect atheistic thought must be credited with a real insight: if existence is a fact, there is no need for a sufficient antecedent reason to account for anything that exists—indeed, there cannot be such a reason. For to argue that there must be a sufficient reason for that which is merely an actual fact, is to suppose that what is actual is more than a fact, that it contains "some necessity." But to suppose this is to go beyond what the facts of experience reveal to us about being.

If we restrict ourselves to the facts we must discard every overt or surreptitious introduction of necessity into the contingency of being. We may not suppose, for instance, that being is contingent only insofar as it is created. For the facts simply tell us that being is contingent—not that there is an exception to this rule, and that, therefore, being may be either contingent or necessary. If we remain consistently empirical, by "being" we can only mean the sort of reality which is revealed in experience—and this reality is as such factual. Therefore, it is not enough to say that *some* being is contingent; we must say that being *as such* is absolutely contingent, and that the expression "necessary being" is a contradiction in terms. Whatever exists, exists contingently—that is, it is a matter of fact.

I stress that this is to be asserted as a matter of fact. The principle that "whatever exists, exists contingently" is not an *a priori* proposition. It does not mean that its universal application results from the prior necessity of the principle. Absolute contingency is universally predicable of being simply because it pertains to being as such—any qualification added to this would reintroduce an *a priori* assumption into our reasoning. For instance, if we were to say: "the being of which we have common or direct experience *does* exist contingently, but the question must be left open whether another order of being escapes this contingency," then the doctrine of the degrees of being would have been reintroduced under the disguise of the distinction between actual and possible being. What is a fact may be asserted universally without the implication that it is more than a matter of fact. (Thus the critique of metaphysics is also the critique of the methodological principle *ab esse ad posse valent consequentia.*)

Likewise, the factuality of being may be asserted universally without the implication that some antecedent necessity (for instance, some metaphysical law of knowledge) requires its assertion. The ambivalence of the factual applies to the fact of consciousness. Man is bound to assert what the facts indicate: to say that the facts are indisputable is to say that we may not dispute them. But it is also true that what is true is not necessarily asserted. The obligation to assert what is true does not come from an antecedent necessity: it is created by the fact that we happened to discover the truth—and this happening is an event, a contingent fact. In sum, conscious existence is no exception to the factuality of being. It tells us nothing new about being. It tells us, however, something very puzzling about man himself: it creates a problem which religious speculation tries to solve.

Man's understanding of being as absolutely contingent creates a problem because man spontaneously understands his own consciousness as the presence of being to itself: man's concept of being is relative to the being which he understands himself to be. Therefore, man understands himself as absolutely contingent in his very human existence. But this involves him in a paradox: consciousness makes man problematic unto himself. Let us now consider the nature of this paradox, and how classical theism and modern atheism have respectively dealt with it.

Man becomes self-problematic because he finds it difficult to reconcile his self-consciousness as being with his being as absolutely contingent fact. Why is this difficult? Evidently, because he can conceive a condition other than absolute contingency which would appear more suitable for him as a self-conscious being. Moreover, this alternative is suggested to him by his consciousness of being as such. For man is aware that, for all the factuality of being and its total lack of meaning in itself, being can be seen by man in a meaningful light insofar as it is interpreted and understood by man. In fact, it *has* to be seen so: man seems unable to stop himself from making sense out of things. This is, to be sure, a strictly relative meaning: it does not imply that being in itself is essentially affected by man's consciousness of it. But man can, as it were, live with being: he can, he must, make sense of it, in relation to himself. This is enough to suggest to him that his own absolute contingency—and, therefore, his own lack of meaning in himself—might be, as it were, made up for, or improved upon.

For consciousness of being does amount to a sort of improvement upon being. As St. Thomas said, "the perfection of each individual thing considered in itself is imperfect. . . . In order that there might be some remedy for this imperfection, another kind of perfection is to be found in created things. It consists in this, that the perfection belonging to one thing is found in another. This is the perfection of a knower insofar as he knows; for something is known by a knower by reason of the fact that the thing known is, in some fashion, in the possession of the knower. . . . In this way it is possible for the perfection of the entire universe to exist in one thing." [2] Thus, though being may lack meaning in itself, man can make it meaningful. Should not man, who is not simply being, but being present to itself, enjoy at least a comparable advantage? In brief: a being cannot very well become aware of its being, as man does, without envisaging the possibility that, despite his absolute contingency, his existence might escape meaninglessness.

The trouble is that the very possibility envisaged as a result of self-consciousness appears to be taken away by the consciousness of oneself as being. The fact that consciousness interprets being and makes it meaningful does not make consciousness to be more than an absolutely contingent fact. The self-problematization of man is indeed paradoxical: the very awareness by which man makes being meaningful, which awakens in him the aspiration to meaningful existence, also makes him aware that he is being—and that, therefore, he lacks meaningful existence in himself. Man makes being meaningful, and yet he has no meaning in himself. He seems unable to do for himself as such what he can do for being as such, despite the fact that he is nothing but being aware of itself as such.

In recent times various forms of atheistic humanism have attempted to solve the problem, noting that man not only interprets being, but can interpret himself as the interpreter of being. I will consider this again below, but I want to remark at this point that, in my opinion, this does not quite solve the problem. It is true that man can give meaning to himself as he understands himself. But this is not enough, because this meaning he gives to himself is, by definition, of the same order as that which he gives to other beings: it is the meaning given by the objectification of being. No doubt, man can understand himself as an object, just as he understands every other being as an object. But this does not give meaning to man as an existent—any more than his objectification of every other being affects that being in any essential way in its actual existence. Man may successfully speculate about himself, philosophically and otherwise—but the success of human speculation is scarcely to be identified with the success of human life. Indeed, human objective self-understanding may even have a dehumanizing effect. The frequent mechanization of human existence in civilized society amply demonstrates that it is possible for man to lose himself in his own objective meaning. Thus, man can disregard the absolute contingency of being in itself and take account, for his own purposes, merely of the meaningfulness of being in relation to man. But in his own case the opposite is true. Man can set aside the relative meaning that he can give to himself when he understands himself (for instance, philosophically or scientifically) as an object among a world of objects, as a being in the world of being. But he cannot very well abstract from his own existence if he wishes to understand himself as he really is. He can hardly disregard, therefore, the absolute contingency of *his* actual experience. It is *that* actual, concrete existence which must be meaningful if man is to be meaningful at all. And it is this sort of meaningfulness that man seems unable to give to himself.

The traditional concept of God as being originates in the supposition that there may well be a supra-human consciousness which might do for man what man can do for another but not for himself. It is not surprising if the more primitive religions pay for this service by saddling themselves with a concept of God who is exactly as arbitrary, pragmatic and exploitative in relation to man, as man is, and rightly so, in relation to being: as the world of being is man's possession, man seems to be God's. The more advanced religions mollify this to some degree or another. But in every case the operative reasoning is that what one being cannot do, a more perfect could do—and, at the end of this trend of thought, that an infinitely perfect being could do it perfectly. For instance, once a self-subsistent source of meaning is supposed, as is done in the doctrine of St. Thomas, it can give meaning not only to man, but to being as such, and human experiences can be understood as merely recovering the meaning put by God into being as such. In any event, both the physical and the metaphysical solutions to the self-problematization of man involve the *a priori* introduction of something at least partly like man himself (namely, something of the order of conscious being), to do what man could envisage himself as doing, if only he were not hampered by limiting circumstances beyond his control.

Perhaps the principal contribution of Kant to religious speculation has been to show that this sort of procedure involves an uncritical use of human reason. But the inestimable contribution of atheism has been to show that it also involves a self-negating contradiction, a self-alienation, of human consciousness.

Atheism has challenged philosophical thought to take seriously the absolute contingency of man, and to follow it through to its ultimate consequences, whatever these may be. For it has taught us that the height of man's actuality, of man's emergence from nothingness, is not measured, as may be that of other beings, by the possibility that he might revert to nothingness. It is measured by the possibility that his emergence from nothingness might turn out to be meaningless—that man's conscious and creative effort to be might turn out to have been expended in vain.

The truth of this insight must be admitted. We must beware of every *arrière pensée*, every suspicion that the recognition of our contingency could be used as the means to avoid facing our self-problematization as we become conscious of our contingency. Throwing ourselves on the mercy of God, as it were, is not likely to change the nature of existence. On the other hand, I am not so certain that atheism does not assume, however subtly, another form of the same gnostic idea I have just described. It is tempting to solve the problem by declaring man absurd, to account for his inability to find meaning in the fact that conscious existence, by the concept of man as absurdity, becomes conscious of itself. Man's self-interpretation as the interpreter of being would seem to yield meaning only if he recognizes that being is absurd.

Yet, this involves what Shubert Ogden has called a "strange witness." [3] The idea that conscious existence is definitively and absolutely absurd is itself an interpretation of man which would define his essential meaning. "If all our actions are in principle absurd," Ogden has argued against Camus, "the act of heroically resisting this absurdity must also be absurd." [4] I would prefer, however, to put it more broadly: if being human is absurd, man's self-definition as absurd must also be absurd. Ultimate meaning cannot be found in ultimate absurdity, as if absurdity accepted ceased to be absurd. In the last analysis, existence stands as a more indisputable and stubborn fact than any conscious attempt to explain it away. Even interpreters of being are what they are only because they exist.

The common inadequacy of atheism and classical theism as

solutions to the self-problematic character of man stems from the idea that if there is a meaning to existence, it must be found within being, within existence itself. The history of philosophy shows how man has run down, one by one, the various ways in which this meaning could be found in being, until only the final, atheistic alternative remained: that it could not be found, because it did not exist. But even this still assumes that, *if* there were a meaning of existence, it would be found in being. However, if this assumption is recognized and avoided, then the history of philosophy holds a different lesson: the meaning of existence cannot indeed be found in being, because it does not exist in being. It may, however, be found elsewhere.

That it is, in fact, found elsewhere is borne out by experience. The self-problematization of man does not imply only man's awareness of the absolute contingency of being. It also implies, I suggest, an awareness that reality transcends being.

The consciousness of being, though revealing only being as the object of experience, places man in a position to question the ultimacy and exclusiveness of being. Consciousness of being as such bestows upon man the capacity to deny and reject being, even while he knows that he himself is involved in this rejection. For instance, consciousness creates in man the possibility of choosing not to exist at all rather than to exist in certain ways. It makes little difference whether we consider a hero's choice to die for a morally worthwhile reason, or a fool's choice to give up his life for a pittance or a whim. In every case, the implication is that existence can be judged by man—indeed, it cannot but be judged by man—once he becomes conscious of it. To the degree that a being becomes conscious of its being, its existence loses its automatic character and demands instead a conscious effort, as it were—and the rejection of existence witnesses to this no less forcefully than does the affirmative choice. Even the choice to drift with existence, or to avoid the encounter with life, implies the self-same requirement of consciousness as it brings man face to face with himself. In the moral order this is reflected in the fact that no one can abdicate his conscience in favor of someone else's judgment unless he *judge* that someone else's judgment is better than his own. All this implies that existence has been put by man into a certain perspective. Its awesome character has been put, as it were, in its proper place. Existence is tamed by thought; it is domesticated by the consideration that, when all is said and done, existence is simply a matter of fact. Thus, if we should ask, with Leibniz, "why is there being rather than nothing?" we are bound to reply: only because a sufficient reason of being exists. But if we ask, "Why shouldn't there be nothing rather than being?" the only reply permitted by empirical reason is: why not, indeed? Is being as such not absolutely contingent? If it is, there is no reason why there should not be nothing rather than something.

But to give this reply is to transcend the assumption that being exhausts reality, that existence marks the totality beyond which only nothing is found. In fact, when we come to think of it, the point is fairly obvious: the very absoluteness of the contingency of being reveals (at least by indirection) that being is not, as it were, the most important, the most significant, the noblest thing in the world. There are things higher than being. What does it profit a man to gain the world of being? For all its value and dignity, all being and all existence, including human existence itself, can be counted for nothing and given up without regret. As the Gospel tradition reminds us, man must not so love existence, even his own, that he does not stand ready, I do not say to accept, but even to embrace, death. If we can understand this, and thus subtract ourselves from any bondage or debt in which we might be held by being on account of our having been born into being, and if we can, thus, thereafter exist freely, as the result of conscious choice, the reason is that we can understand ourselves in the light of that which transcends being in every way.

I have said that the contingency of being reveals this at least by indirection, because our awareness of the contingency of being does not altar the fact that it is being, not that which transcends being, which is the object of human thought. If we can so easily misconceive what our religious experience reveals, the reason is that being is and remains the object of conscious experience. That which transcends being is revealed only *in* being, and *within* the experience of being, in the sense that our experience of being, and only our experience of being, reveals in us the capacity to judge being (whether rightly or not) and to dispose of it (whether for good or for ill). Though conscious being is conscious of being, and though it is conscious of no object but being, in the consciousness of its object, namely, being, it can become conscious of that which is not an object, namely, that which transcends being. In this sense, man's consciousness of being is not bound by being: consciousness is not enclosed by that which it itself is, or by that object which it is conscious of. Thus, since being remains the object of consciousness even after the disclosure of the reality which transcends it, every conceptualization of that which transcends being is necessarily relative to being: the very concept I have used constantly here, "a reality which transcends being," is the most obvious instance of this.

Nevertheless, our experience of being reveals that which transcends being, even if it reveals it in relation to being. This is why the disclosure of that which transcends being is at the same time also the disclosure of man's deepest reality to himself. In this sense, awareness of the reality which transcends being is what reveals to man the meaning of existence. But this formula is somewhat equivocal: what it really reveals is that the meaning of existence is not to be found within existence itself, but beyond. Moreover, since being remains the object of experience, this revelation has a peculiar character given to it by a certain quality. I refer, of course, to the quality of faith. The affirmation that existence is meaningful only in relation to that which transcends existence—and the affirmation of that which transcends existence requires faith, because it is the affirmation of that in relation to which man understands himself as having a meaningfulness which he does not have in himself.

For these reasons, among the various ways in which we may conceptualize positively that reality which transcends being, "presence" seems to me particularly apt. Presence signifies that which in its very otherness is related to one. We say, for instance, that someone is of good presence if his bearing seems striking to us. A foreign power is present in the former colony if, despite the latter's newly acquired independence, it still helps fashion its culture and policies. And another human being is genuinely present to us, and not merely as a matter of geographical location, if he makes us come alive, if he brings out our best—or, for that matter, our worst—self, if he contributes significantly, for good or for ill, to the emergence of our selves. But is this not what God does for man, namely, to reveal him to himself in a dimension which would otherwise remain altogether closed to him? Actually, I have put it backwards. We should rather say: Does being not reveal itself most meaningfully to itself, and does consciousness not become most fully itself, because the presence of being to itself takes place in the presence of an order of reality which transcends being itself?

Religious experience, then, does not reveal a transcendent being: what it reveals is that being exists in a presence which transcends it. To conceptualize in the contradictory terms of transcendent being the belief made possible by the awareness of absolute contingency may well have been unavoidable at a certain level of the evolution of human consciousness. But to conceive it in terms of transcendent presence to being may be more adequate today.

I have already alluded to a possible misinterpretation of these suggestions. A transcendent presence, a reality which transcends being, does not imply that the concept of "transcendent presence" or the concept of "a reality which transcends being" should *substitute* for the concept of being in metaphysics. A metaphysics of "presence" or of "reality" would be either a fraud or an equivocation if it were but a metaphysics of being in disguise. The objection which can be levelled at metaphysics is not that it is concerned with being *qua* being, but that it understands being as such uncritically and *a priori*. Hence, I must insist that neither presence nor reality is that to which, rather than to being, "the intellect reduces all its concepts." [5] For once the reducibility of every reality to being is presupposed, we have entered the path of metaphysics, having thereby presupposed that in the unity of the concept of being can be reconciled the variety of degrees of the reality

107

of being. But, likewise, to suppose that presence, or reality, or anything else, would reconcile in the unity of the concept the variety of empirical and trans-empirical realities, would be to enter into the same metaphysical path, with but the difference that one's shoes would have been resoled. The doctrine of the degrees of being is scarcely transcended if it is simply replaced by the doctrine of the degrees of presence or the degrees of reality.

It is little to be doubted that we do experience being as the reality of the world and of ourselves. But to go beyond this empirical fact and invest being with a transcendental character is gratuitously and *a priori* to impose upon any possible transcendental reality a preconception which may be harmless only as long as it is not pursued to its bitter end. For atheism, which is in part a protest against the prejudicial confusion of being and reality, is also in part a consequence of it. As we invest being as such with a transcendental character we close ourselves off to the possibility of experiencing any reality other than that of the world and of ourselves. Metaphysics has had, in effect, the unbargained-for result of placing God beyond all possible experience. But, like the luminiferous aether, a metaphysical God ultimately became superfluous and had to be either discarded or else irrationally believed. In this as in other respects, the traces of the great contributions of Greek, medieval and modern philosophy to human thought can be found within the most progressive, but also within the most anti-Christian, aspects of contemporary thought.

NOTES

1. *Summa Theologica*, Ia, q. 86, a. 3.
2. *De Veritate*, q. 2, a. 2.
3. Shubert Ogden, *The Reality of God* (New York: Harper and Row, 1966), pp. 120 ff.
4. *Ibid.*, p. 41.
5. *De Veritate*, q. 1, a. 1.

GOD'S PSEUDONYMS

Robert McAfee Brown

THE LANGUAGE ABOUT GOD THESE DAYS tends to be a curious combination of modesty and extravagance—modesty at how little some people claim to know about Him, extravagance at the degree of assurance with which others claim we can know little or nothing. To some, of course, God is still totally and triumphantly *present*, and a noted evangelist can rebut the charge that God is dead by countering, "I know that God is alive, because I talked with Him this morning," a response that effectively stops further pursuit of the point.

But the mood is generally more chastened. Ever since the time of Isaiah, and probably before him, men have spoken of God as *hidden*, and Pascal was not the only one to echo Isaiah's plaintive cry, "Truly, thou art a God who hidest thyself." [1] Martin Buber has spoken of the *eclipse* of God, another dramatic image, but has insisted that in spite of this eclipse, brought about in part at least by man's sin, we must seek to redeem the word that has fallen into such disrepute. "We cannot cleanse the word 'God' and we cannot make it whole," he writes, "but, defiled and mutilated as it is, we can raise it from the ground and set it over an hour of great care." [2]

In our day the notion of the *absence* of God has gained much currency: there may be a God, but if so, the evidence of His presence is so agonizingly slim that we must discount the possibility that He will reappear in our time. Until He does, we must, in Gabriel Vahanian's words, "Wait without idols." [3] This theme seems new and rather daring, but it may in fact be little more than a refinement of the deistic notion, not of the absent God, but of the absentee God, the one who was once around but has now retired to the sidelines, leaving the universe to run its own course, virtually independent of Him.

Even more extravagant than these images, of course, is the contemporary theme of the *death* of God, although it is not always clear what the proponents of this theme mean. Sometimes they mean that the idea of God, as a theme of human contemplation and commitment, has died, and that the term is thus a description of our cultural situation rather than a metaphysical or ontological statement.[4] Many of them find the news curiously liberating and seem unimpressed with Rabbi Richard Rubenstein's disavowal of such optimism: "The death of God as a cultural phenomenon is undeniable," he comments, "but this is no reason to dance at the funeral." Others, however, press beyond this phenomenological statement to the assertion that God really and truly has died, that this death is an historical event, and that it took a so-called Christian civilization about nineteen centuries to catch up with the truth. But even those who most buoyantly proclaim God's death go on to insist that there has been a kind of resurrection of God in a new form, as the epiphany of new possibilities for a humanity now liberated from false and outworn beliefs.[5]

In connection with this last position, I happen to be among those who believe that the reports of God's death, like the initial reports of Mark Twain's, have been somewhat exaggerated, and I agree with the editors of *New Theology No. 4* that the so-called "death of God theology" was a phenomenon already passing from the theological scene when it was belatedly discovered by *Time, Newsweek, Playboy,* and other representatives of the mass media.[6] I do not therefore intend in what follows to flail a dead horse, let alone a dead God. These modes of speech in our day which speak of God as present, hidden, eclipsed, absent or dead, are, I say, extravagant modes of speech. I do not use the term pejoratively, but descriptively, and partly as a means of setting off by contrast the more modest and less extravagant task in which I propose to engage. For I want to deal with the more circumscribed theme of God's pseudonyms, the "strange names" I believe him to be using in our time.

This theme suggests that to the degree that God is *present*, it may mean that He is present in a strange way, and that the usual criteria for measuring His presence may have to be revised. To the degree that God is *hidden*, it may mean that He has chosen to hide himself (as Isaiah suspected) so that we are forced to search Him out in unlikely places. To the degree that He is in *eclipse*, it may be that the shadows bringing about the eclipse can force us to survey the once-familiar terrain from new perspectives, and finally to see it with greater clarity than was possible for us when it was fully bathed in the sunshine of an undisturbed faith. To the degree that God is *absent*, it may be that such absence is His self-imposed catalyst to force us into acknowledging fresh modes for His apprehension. And to the degree that He is *dead*—but here, of course, the comparative mode of speech breaks down, for it is not possible to speak of degrees of "deadness" (though with some of the things theologians say these days, I would not put it past someone to try). The death of God as a description of a cultural phenomenon, however, can be so described, and to the degree that our notion of God has suffered mortal blows, this may in fact be precisely the prerequisite for a genuine resurrection in our experience of the true God, purged of at least some of the confining and distorting notions we have tried to attach to Him. And for this task of trying to make ourselves open once again to the reality of one whose dimensions we cannot measure, and whom eye cannot see nor ear hear, the imagery of the pseudonym may be of some use.

I

The theme was first suggested to me in the very moving novel of Ignazio Silone, called *Bread and Wine*.[7] The novel tells the story of Pietro Spina, a communist revolutionary in Italy in the 1930s during the rise of Italian fascism, the period in which Mussolini waged his savage war against Ethiopia. Spina is concerned to discern the signs of the times, and an elderly priest, Don Benedetto, who had been his teacher, makes the rather startling remark to him:

> In times of conspiratorial and secret struggle, the Lord is obliged to hide Himself and assume pseudonyms. Besides, and you know it, He does not attach very much importance to His name. . . . Might not the ideal of social justice that animates the masses today be one of the pseudonyms the Lord is using to free Himself from the control of the churches and the banks? [8]

To get the full force of this statement, it must be realized that "the ideal of social justice that animates the masses" in Italy in the 1930s, to which the priest was referring, was communism. Don Benedetto was saying, in other words, that the hand of God might be more clearly discerned among the Italian communists than among the Italian priests or bankers.

Initially this seems a strange idea, perhaps even a demonic idea. It seems strange that a God who presumably wants to enter into fellowship with His children should show Himself not directly but indirectly, and it seems demonic that the vehicle through which He should indirectly show Himself—the pseudonym or false name He should use—would be something so apparently antithetical to His purposes as communism. But Don Benedetto, as he pursues his theme, makes clear that there is nothing new in this idea. It has, in fact, a long history.

> This would not be the first time that the Eternal Father felt obligated to hide Himself and take a pseudonym. As you know, He has never taken the first name and the last name men have fastened on Him very seriously; quite to the contrary, He has warned men not to name Him in vain as His first commandment. And then, the Scriptures are full of clandestine life. Have you ever considered the real meaning of the flight into Egypt? And later, when he was an adult, was not Jesus forced several times to hide himself and flee from the Judeans? [9]

Don Benedetto also instances Elijah's experience in the desert, to which we shall presently turn, and Silone himself is so caught up with this theme that in his stage version of *Bread and Wine* he renames the story, *And He Did Hide Himself*,[10] developing even more prominently through the mouthpiece of Friar Giochinno the notion that Jesus Himself had to assume pseudonyms, another theme to which we shall presently turn. We may push the matter a bit further, therefore, not only in terms of Silone's use of the theme, but also in terms of his insistence that this is not a new theme but an old one, and that it is indeed a consistent Biblical theme as well.

II

Three Old Testament examples of the theme of God's use of pseudonyms may be suggested as the foundation for a further consideration of its possible contemporary usefulness. The first of these occurs in Genesis 28:10–17. Jacob is *en route* from Beersheba to Haran. Night comes, and so he camps along the road, stopping at what is described as "a certain place" to spend the night. There is nothing special about this place at all. It is not a shrine, it is not a holy place, it is not the goal of the day's journey. It is simply where Jacob happens to be when the sun goes down. During the night he has a dream about a ladder from earth to heaven, upon which angels are ascending and descending.[11] What is important for our present purposes is neither the dream nor the content of the dream, but the comment that Jacob makes when he awakes, since it becomes almost a paradigm of the experience of the pseudonymity of God. The next morning Jacob makes two statements, both of which are very true: first, "Surely the Lord is in this place," as indeed He was; second, "I did not know it," as indeed he did not (cf. Genesis 28:16). God's presence was not dependent upon Jacob's perception of that presence—a fact from which we can derive some comfort when we today too readily identify the reality or existence of God with our own degree of perception of His reality or existence. But even more important, I believe, was the fact that the reality of that presence came home to Jacob in a quite unexpected place and set of circumstances. Jacob did not discover God in a shrine or place of worship, but far from any such place. He did not discover Him in the midst of any cultic exercise or act of mercy. He did not suddenly in the midst of

113

prayer experience the healing reality of God's presence. No, it was in the totally unexpected event of setting up camp in the desert, in the midst of a tedious journey, that God manifested Himself in a strange way. How strange and irregular this was to Jacob's experience is rather perversely attested to by the fact that Jacob's reaction was precisely to build a shrine on that spot, to try to regularize the unexpected experience, to divest the experience of its pseudonymity and make it predictable, calculable and manageable.

A second Biblical example of God's use of pseudonyms is one to which Don Benedetto himself makes oblique reference in his conversation with Spina, and one that is recounted in 1 Kings 19:1–12. A little later in Israel's history Elijah is also leaving Beersheba, only this time he is not making a calculated journey: he is fleeing from that very domineering queen named Jezebel who is after his neck. So Elijah flees to the wilderness. Yahweh pursues him and orders him to stand upon the mount before the Lord. "Before the Lord": but how will Elijah know the presence of the Lord? The account continues:

And behold, the LORD passed by, and a great and strong wind rent the mountains, and broke in pieces the rocks before the LORD, but the LORD was not in the wind; and after the wind an earthquake, but the LORD was not in the earthquake; and after the earthquake a fire, but the LORD was not in the fire; and after the fire a still, small voice. . . .[12]

The Lord strong and mighty was not in the wind. The Lord of heaven and earth was not in the earthquake. The Lord of all power was not in the fire. Recall that these means—earthquake, wind and fire—were the normal ways through which a man in Elijah's time would have expected a theophany of the divine presence. But no, after these usual manifestations of the divine comes "a still, small voice," or as one translator has put it, "the sound of a soft stillness." [13] And it was in "the sound of a soft stillness" that the God of earthquake, wind and fire was present —the last place on earth in which Elijah would have expected to find Him. Once again, God is working through the unexpected, and confronting man not in the normal way but in a strange way, through pseudonymous activity.

A third example of this strange activity of God occurs still later in Israel's history, recounted in that curious and disturbing passage in Isaiah 10:5–19. Isaiah is rightly worried because Israel is paying no attention to Yahweh's demands. He feels that Yahweh is about to engage in a mighty manifestation of His sovereign power. And he links this with the fact that Assyria, a great pagan world power—today we would say a "secular" world power—is poised on the northern borders about to invade the land of God's people, the Jews. Isaiah feels that the power of Yahweh will be manifested in the ensuing battle. Now the customary thing to assume in such situations was that God would, of course, work through His chosen people. They who were to be a "light unto the Gentiles" would surely be the vehicle through which the strong right arm of Yahweh would be manifested to the Gentiles.

But Isaiah did not say that at all. Instead, he said the scandalous and shocking thing that God's instrument would be the pagan Assyria, and that it would be through Assyrian power that God would show forth His will. Assyria, of course, did not know that it was being used by God, and did not even acknowledge the existence of God. Indeed, Assyria would later claim that it had won the victory by the power of its own strong arm, and would scoff at the notion that it was the instrument of Yahweh. But nevertheless, so Isaiah asserts, it will be by means of Assyria that God will declare His will to His people Israel. Once again, God uses a strange name. He does not use the name of His people, Israel; He uses the name of a pagan people, Assyria. Assyria, not Israel, becomes "the rod of His anger, the staff of His fury," and the "godless people" against whom Assyria is sent, is paradoxically the very people of God.

There are three instances, taken almost at random, of a theme that could be reproduced many times over from the Old Testament. They illustrate that God can use whatever means He chooses, whatever means are to hand—a rest stop on a trip, the calm after a storm, the hosts of the pagans—in order to communicate His will to His people. His ways of working are not limited to the ways people expect Him to work, and He clearly refuses to be bound by man's ideas of how He ought to behave. Notice, too, one other thing about these examples. They illustrate three classic ways in which men have claimed to "find God"—through *personal experience* (in the case of Jacob), through *nature* (in the case of Elijah), and through *history* (in the case of Isaiah). In each case, indeed, a confrontation takes place between man and God, but in each case it takes place in an unexpected way. The personal experience is not the personal experience of worship or some other conventional means of encountering God. The confrontation in nature is through the vehicle of nature least expected to produce such a confrontation. The lesson read from history is the lesson least expected and the hardest to accept. In each case, God uses a pseudonym, a strange name, and upsets all human calculations.

III

Let us accept, then, Don Benedetto's theme that God is sometimes obliged to hide Himself and assume pseudonyms, and that He does not attach very much importance to His name. The name men conventionally attach to Him may now be an empty name, the place men look for Him may now be the place He is not, and the places men fail to look may be precisely the locations in which His hidden activity is most apparent to those who look with eyes of faith. Where, then, do we find signs of His pseudonymous activity today? Are we to look for Him *only* in strange places? I do not believe so. To say that He acts pseudonymously does not mean He can never be found in His Church, but it will surely mean that He is not confined to His Church. To say that He acts pseudonymously does not mean that His light no longer shines through the saints, but it will surely mean that His saints are more numerous and found in more unlikely places than we are usually inclined to acknowledge. To say that He acts pseudonymously does not mean that Scripture is no longer useful in discerning His hidden ways (and the instances just cited should be supporting evidence enough for that), but it will surely mean that other

116

literature as well is a vehicle for discerning His veiled presence, not only in Silone, who knows the lineaments of a Christian faith he cannot directly profess himself, but in a host of other writers who plumb the depths of the human predicament with a sensitivity not found in most contemporary pulpits.[14]

To try to discern the signs of the presence of pseudonymous God in the world today is surely a risky business, but the risk must be taken if we are not to leave our thesis irrelevantly suspended in mid-air. I therefore offer now two examples of places where I see signs of His activity more compelling to me than the conventional modes of His expression that theologians normally delight to trace, and to sharpen the issue I shall state these in deliberately provocative terms.

The first example of this pseudonymous activity of God in our present age is in the agitation and demonstration in which our country has been engaged in the field of civil rights for minority groups. The white churches, to their shame, have not been very active in this struggle. One does not look to those who call themselves "God's own people" for leadership in this matter. There has been little significant indication that many white Christians have really been concerned about the indignities that they and other white people have visited upon the black people of this country for the last three hundred years. If we are to be honest, we must acknowledge that the real battle has been carried on by the secular groups, or by the Negro church groups, but not by the white church groups. Whatever advances have been won in the cause of social justice have been won either in the face of white Christian apathy or white Christian opposition. As the late Martin Luther King forcefully and correctly put it, "What is disturbing is not the appalling actions of the bad people, but the appalling silence of the good people." Such an indictment must be accepted not merely as a justifiable cry of outrage, but as a simple descriptive statement.

Now let us face it. We do not usually expect to see the hand of the Lord in secular groups, in mass meetings, in public demonstrations, in picket lines, in sit-ins, in civil disobedience, in people being herded off to jail, in court rooms, and all the rest. But can we escape the fact that those are the places and activities through which concern for the fact that *all* men are God's children is being expressed today? And that the same fact is not expressed, but denied, in the white communities with written or unwritten covenants of closed occupancy, or the white churches with the token Negro tenor prominently displayed in the choir? No, the Lord is in those strange places, and, like Jacob, we have not known it.

The tragedy has been that we have not learned it soon enough, and that, because of *our* blindness and callousness and indifference, the incredible patience of non-violent Negro discipline has turned to violence. The white community cannot blame the black community for the urban riots of the summer of 1967, and the fearful portent of more to come in succeeding summers. The white community, holding all the power, has done too little, too late, and forced the despairing outcry that finally has exhausted any hope of working through the white-dominated political process, and turns now in total frustration to all that is left—the brick, the stick, the fire, the bullet.[15] Is not a word of the Lord being spoken through all this, that the longer we flout the demand for justice and mercy, the heavier will be the penalties we have to pay? Let us learn to listen, through the anguished cries of the dispossessed in the ghettoes, to the insistent word, the ground bass theme of all the history of exploitation of one group by another, "Let my people go."

To me the most haunting line in contemporary literature occurs in the exchange between Msimangu and Kumalo, the two black priests in Alan Paton's book, *Cry, the Beloved Country*. They are talking about the white man. And Msimangu says to Kumalo, "I have one great fear in my heart, that one day when they are turned to loving they will find that we are turned to hating." [16] So insistent is the theme that Paton has Kumalo recall it a second time at the very end of the book: "When they turn to loving they will find we are turned to hating." [17] It is already possible that this could become the epitaph of our nation. And the question is: can we hear this as the insistent clamor of the pseudonymous God in our day, addressed to us, warning us, "Do not look for me just in the sanctuaries, or in the precise words of theologians, or in the calm of the country-side; look for me in the place where men are struggling for their very survival as human beings, where they are heaving off the load of centuries of degradation, where they are insisting that the rights of the children of God are the rights of all my children and not just some; and if you will not find me there, expect to find me acting in more heavy-handed fashion elsewhere."

There is a second place where I see the pseudonymous God at work in our nation today. This is at the moment a more "controversial" issue, just as a few years ago civil rights was more controversial than it is now. But the fact that it is more controversial does not deter me, for I have a conviction that wherever God turns up, pseudonymously or not, He provokes controversy, since He challenges what is going on. (Let us not suppose that Isaiah's suggestion that Assyria, and not Israel, had become God's instrument went unchallenged; he was probably lucky to escape with his life.) I believe that God is using His "strange name" in trying to tell us something desperately important through the rising voice of protest about American involvement in Vietnam. I do not intend to turn this discussion into a treatment of the intricacies of American foreign policy, but it would be the height of hypocrisy as well as the expression of a lack of even minimal moral courage, to try to sidestep the issue, since it is the most burning moral issue of this decade.[18]

That there is something wrong about the most powerful nation on earth systematically destroying a tiny nation ought long ago to have been crystal clear to everyone, but it has not been. Dropping napalm on women and children and the aged, so that peoples' chins melt into their chests, ought long ago to have aroused in us the height of moral indignation, but it has not. That we justify our presence in Vietnam in the name of opposing a monolithic "world communism" that began to crumble over a decade ago, ought long ago to have made us demand a stern accounting of our leaders, but it has not. That we are entitled to impose our will wherever we wish in the world, supporting military dictatorships that do not represent their people, ought long ago to have made us cry out in protest, but it has not. "Destroying a city in order to save it," as an American officer described our destruction of Ben Tre, ought to impress us as a hideous example of Orwellian doublethink, but it does not.

Once more, we must concede that the churches have been relatively silent on this issue. After one has mentioned the late Archbishop Hallinan, Bishop Shannon, Bishop Sheen, Bishop Dougherty and one or two others, he can count on the fingers of one hand the American Roman Catholic bishops who have publicly felt a sense of moral ambiguity about American presence in Vietnam. With a few individual exceptions, the top-brass leadership in Protestantism, Orthodoxy and Judaism has been similarly reticent about a real probe of the morality of mass killing in the name of the high-sounding ideals our State Department once avowed, and has now abandoned in the name of a tough-minded policy of national self-interest, which even on those terms can be rebutted as self-defeating. The churches, the "godly," have had an incredible timidity in this matter. Would that American Roman Catholic bishops went even as far as the South Vietnamese Roman Catholic bishops, who asked for a cessation of the bombing of North Vietnam even as the American military forces, with the implicit support of most churchmen, continued the senseless destruction around Hanoi which the former Secretary of Defense himself said did not succeed.

Where has the voice of moral outrage come from? Not from churches, not from business, not from labor. No, it has come from the students, who on this issue have displayed considerably greater moral sensitivity than their elders. They have helped to remind the rest of us that national pride and arrogance are things in which they take no pride, and for which their generation is not willing to kill dark-skinned peoples thousands of miles away. And we are witnessing an escalation of moral protest in response to the escalation of military power, as students across the land are trying to tell the older generation that the war we are fighting is both futile and immoral. Many from both generations may not like some of the stridency of voice and action that accompanies the protest, but it has been our deafness that has made the stridency necessary, and woe to those of any generation who do not hear in this anguished protest a strong note of moral urgency.

If in this situation, I look for a sign of the pseudonymous God at work, do I find it in an administration that has in fact committed itself to a policy that anything is permissible to achieve military victory? I do not. I find it much more in the words of dozens of young men I have talked to, and thousands more across the land, who say, "I will not kill my fellow man, even if it means five years in prison"; who say, "If America intends to police the world, it will first have to imprison its youth." I find it also in the commitment of those in public life who are willing to pay a great price to speak against the madness that has seized our nation's leaders. These voices are few indeed, in comparison to the rest who by silence or inactivity condone our slaughter of the Vietnamese, and there are times when I wonder whether human madness may not stifle and destroy the presence of God.

In such a mood, I turn back to Silone, and discover that Don Benedetto faced the same question himself, and that the analogies to the Italian war in Ethiopia, to which the aged priest refers, and the American war in Vietnam become more congruent with each passing hour. Don Benedetto ruminates:

I, too, in the dregs of my affliction, have asked myself: Where is God and why has He abandoned us? Certainly the loud-speakers and bells announcing the new slaughter were not God. Nor were the cannon shots and the bombing of Ethiopian villages, of which we read every day in the newspapers. But if one poor man gets up in the middle of the night and writes on the walls of the village with a piece of charcoal or varnish, "Down with the War," the presence of God is undoubtedly behind that man. How can one not recognize the divine light in his scorn of danger and in his love for the so-called enemies? Thus, if some simple workmen are condemned for these reasons by a special tribunal, there's no need to hesitate to know where God stands.[19]

That the manner of contemporary protest against the war is disquieting is no sign that God is absent. Indeed, we can expect that God's presence, in whatever form, will be disquieting. We will find Him not just where there is peace, but where there is turmoil; not just where things are calm, but where things are stirred up.

IV

It is a temptation to stop right there. One could surely argue that a case has been made: God can work in unexpected ways, employ pseudonyms, and we have now seen instances of this not only in biblical history but in our own contemporary history. Q.E.D. But one must not succumb to the temptation to stop right there. For out of a number of questions that could be raised, particularly about the immediately preceding paragraphs, there is one surely that must be faced, whatever others are to be omitted. This is the question: how can one be sure that it is *God* who is working in these various ways and not someone or something else? Is not this whole approach likely to make God simply capricious, not really trustworthy or knowable, to be looked for merely in the bizarre or the curious circumstance? Or to focus the question even more bluntly: do we not simply pick our own pet social hobbies and try to invest them with ultimate moral worth by saying that they are the activities through which God is working? Are we not simply trying to enlist God on our side? How can we be so sure God is working through the pseudonyms that just happen to appeal to us?

That is a fair question. (It can be asked, I have discovered from personal experience, in considerably less genteel ways and with considerably more venom behind it.) Let me try to indicate the guidelines along which I think it can be answered. The answer involves, for me at any rate, a shift from the Old Testament material to the New Testament, though I think an answer congruent to the one I am suggesting is to a high degree possible on Old Testament terms as well.

If we want to find a criterion in terms of which to discern where God is or is not employing pseudonyms today, I think we find it in relation to the time and place where God did show us most clearly who He is and how He makes Himself known to us. Any other attempt to trace His activity must be tested against how adequately they reflect what we know of Him from that central event. The time, of course, is the first thirty years of what we now call the Christian era, though it presupposes the many generations of Jewish history preceding it. The place is that tiny little strip of land known as Palestine, tucked off in a corner of the Roman Empire. And the important thing for our present concern is that this event likewise underlines the unexpectedness of the divine activity, the sense in which here too God used a pseudonym, the sense in which here too His activity was just as strange and unexpected as in the case of Jacob, Elijah or Isaiah, the sense in which all that came to fulfillment in the life of Jesus of Nazareth is simply contrary to the way any of us would have written the script.

Kierkegaard puts the theme most strongly when he reminds us that it is not possible to understand who Jesus of Nazareth is unless we have gone through the possibility of offense at the claims that center on Him. We must be offended at the notion that God would work through the son of a lower-class carpenter who may well have been illiterate. What else can we be but offended? Only if we have genuinely entertained the possibility, Kierkegaard insists, that God would work in such a strange way, with such a strange name as Jeshua bar-Josef, can we go beyond offense to affirmation.[20]

Let me seek, if possible, to drive the point home by the following device: Suppose, just for a moment, that we were waiting now for some tremendous manifestation of God's activity. Suppose that it had been promised that God would intervene in our human situation, and that it was now clear that the time was at hand. Where would we look for Him? Where would we expect that God would manifest Himself? Surely, the answer would be, in one of the great nations, where as many people as possible would be exposed to this important fact; surely in a well-established family with much influence; surely in such a way that all the resources of public opinion and mass media could be used to acquaint people with what happened; surely it would be the most public and open and widely accessible event possible.

But in terms of the way the New Testament reports it happening back then, if it were to happen today, I think it would be more like this: A child would be born into a backward South African tribe, the child of poor parents with almost no education. He would grow up under a government that would not acknowledge his right to citizenship. During his entire lifetime he would travel no more than about fifty miles from the village of his birth, and would spend most of that lifetime simply following his father's trade—a hunter, perhaps, or a primitive farmer. He would, toward the end, begin to gather a few followers together, talking about things that sounded so dangerous to the authorities that the police would finally move in and arrest him, at which point his following would collapse and his friends would fade back into their former jobs and situations. After a short time in prison and a rigged trial he would be shot by the prison guards as an enemy of the state.

I submit that most of us would find it hard to take seriously the claim that such an event was the most important manifestation of God that men ever had, or were going to have in the future. That would indeed appear to be a pseudonymous act, with the emphasis on the "pseudo-", the false. And yet that is precisely what the attitude of almost any first-century person must have been to the assertion that the Son of God had been born in a cowstall in tiny Bethlehem and that he was, of all things, a lower-class Jew, whose parents became refugees, and who had Himself to go into hiding on several occasions. If on other occasions the common people heard Him gladly,[21] when it came to the showdown and there was a kind of first-century "demonstration" in the streets of Jerusalem, they quickly shifted their "hosannas" to cries of "crucify Him." [22]

And yet those episodes, and others like them, are the very stuff out of which the Christian claim is created. Jesus of Nazareth becomes God's unexpected way of acting, God's pseudonym, and He becomes the norm or pattern in terms of which we are to believe that God will continue to act. So if it strikes us as strange today that God should be working through Negroes in cities, or through students who for reasons of conscience defy a law, or through groups that are not part of the religious establishment, such assertions are at least consistent with the strange way God acted back then through One who was looked upon as a criminal, spat upon and despised, and finally strung up in the midst of the city dump heap.

In different periods of history men emphasize different portions of those gospel accounts, and surely for our age, with its concern for the extension of justice to those to whom it has been denied, the Christological theme that Bonhoeffer stresses of Jesus as "the Man for others" is an inescapable theme.[23] Since He was an outcast, we must not be surprised to find contemporary reflections of His presence among the outcast. Since He was a servant, we must look for signs of His presence today among those who serve. Since He was part of an oppressed minority, we must expect to hear the echo of His voice today among those who are oppressed. In an era when many men have no place to call their own, we must expect a response of resonating concern from One who had nowhere to lay His head. Since two-thirds of the world goes to bed hungry each night, we must recall the One who made available not only spiritual comfort but solid and tangible loaves and fishes.

Since He became man, we must acknowledge that in every man there is one who can be served in His name, just as He served all men in His Father's name. Since He lived very much in the world, we will look for Him not only in holy places or by means of holy words, but will look for Him also in the very common, ordinary things of life for which He gave Himself: bread (whether broken around a kitchen table or at an altar), carpentry, men in need, even tax collectors. In a time when men suffer, we will not be surprised to discover that He suffered also, nor will we flinch when Bonhoeffer pronounces the initially disturbing words, "Only the suffering God can help." [24] And we will find also, in that strange paradox of which Bonhoeffer also speaks, that in the very midst of God-forsakenness, which Jesus too experienced, we thereby discover the presence of God even in the place that is defined as His absence.[25]

In one of her plays about the nativity, Dorothy Sayers sums up this theme. One of the three kings is describing what it would mean to him, if one could take seriously the staggering possibility that God deigns to stoop to identify Himself with man. And he goes on:

I do not mind being ignorant and unhappy—
All I ask is the assurance that I am not alone,
Some courage, some comfort against this burden of fear and pain.
. . . I look out between the strangling branches of the vine and see
Fear in the east, fear in the west; armies
And banners marching and garments rolled in blood.
Yet this is nothing, if only God will not be indifferent,
If He is beside me, bearing the weight of His own creation,
If I may hear His voice among the voices of the vanquished,
If I may feel His hand touch mine in the darkness,
If I may look upon the hidden face of God
And read in the eyes of God
That He is acquainted with grief.[26]

That, I suppose, is the ultimate in the pseudonymous activity of God—that He should be acquainted with grief. And yet that appears to be the place where we must look for Him today. In his parable of the King and the maiden, Kierkegaard makes response as follows, to the claim that in Jesus the God incarnate is present:

The servant-form is no mere outer garment, and therefore the God must suffer all things, endure all things, make experience of all things. He must suffer hunger in the desert, he must thirst in the time of his agony, he must be forsaken in death, absolutely like the humblest—behold the man! His suffering is not that of his death, but this entire life is a story of suffering; and it is love that suffers, the love which gives all is itself in want.[27]

So the point of greatest clarity is the point of greatest incongruity and surprise. Jesus Himself is the grand pseudonym, the supreme instance of God acting in ways contrary to our expectation, the point at which we are offered the criterion in terms of which the action of God elsewhere can be measured. And if we miss His presence in the world, it will not be because He is not there, but simply because we have been looking for Him in the wrong places.

NOTES

1. Isaiah 45:15. Pascal picks up the theme in *Pensées*, #194, 242.
2. Martin Buber, *Eclipse of God* (New York: Harper, 1952), p. 18.
3. Cf. Gabriel Vahanian, *Wait Without Idols* (New York: Braziller, 1964). I have explored the notion from a different perspective in "The Theme of Waiting in Modern Literature," *Ramparts*, Summer 1964, 68–75, dealing with Beckett, Kafka and Auden.
4. Cf. Vahanian, *The Death of God* (New York: Braziller, 1961), and writings from William Hamilton's "middle period" such as *The New Essence of Christianity* (New York: Association Press, 1961).
5. The literature is endless. Cf. *inter alia*, Altizer and Hamilton, *Radical Theology and the Death of God* (Indianapolis: Bobbs-Merrill, 1966), and Altizer, *The Gospel of Christian Atheism* (Philadelphia: Westminster, 1966), for first-hand expositions.
6. Cf. Marty and Peerman, eds., *New Theology No. 4* (New York: Macmillan, 1967), esp. pp. 9–15.
7. Ignazio Silone, *Bread and Wine* (New York: Athenaeum, 1962), a revision of an earlier form of the novel published in America by Penguin (New York, 1946). I have developed Silone's use of the theme more fully in "Ignazio Silone and the Pseudonyms of God," a contribution to a symposium to be published by the University of Pittsburgh Press.
8. Silone, *op. cit.* (Penguin), pp. 247–248. Silone's later revision does not contain the quotation in this precise form.
9. Silone, *op. cit.* (Athenaeum), p. 274.
10. Silone, *And He Did Hide Himself* (London: Jonathan Cape, 1946).
11. I forego the tempting possibility of dealing with dreams as unlikely vehicles of the divine presence, enticing though that might be on another occasion.
12. 1 Kings 19:11–12.
13. Cf. Brewer, *The Literature of the Old Testament* (New York: Columbia University Press, 1938), p. 48.

14. On this theme, cf. *inter alia* such recent writings from diverse viewpoints as Scott, *The Broken Center* (New Haven: Yale University Press, 1965); TeSelle, *Literature and the Christian Life* (New Haven: Yale University Press, 1966); and Axthelm, *The Modern Confessional Novel* (New Haven: Yale University Press, 1967).

15. These words were written before the release of the Presidential Advisory Commission's Report on Civil Disorders. This "secular" document insists, in hard-hitting terms, that the reason for the riots is not black conspiracy, but "white racism." Cf. *Report of the National Advisory Commission on Civil Disorders*, with an introduction by Tom Wicker (New York: Bantam Books, 1968). The document is a splendid example of the voice of the pseudonymous God speaking in our time.

16. Alan Paton, *Cry, the Beloved Country* (New York: Scribners, 1948), pp. 39–40.

17. *Ibid.*, p. 272.

18. No one hopes more than the author that the material that follows will soon become dated. But this only underlines the central thesis of the chapter, that God must be looked for in contemporaneous events and not only in generalities.

19. Silone, *Bread and Wine*, pp. 275–276.

20. Cf. further on this theme, Kierkegaard, *Training in Christianity* (Princeton: Princeton University Press, 1941), esp. Part II, pp. 79–144.

21. Cf. Mark 12:37.

22. Cf. the shift between Matthew 21:9 and Matthew 27:22–23.

23. Cf. Bonhoeffer, *Letters and Papers from Prison* (New York: Macmillan, 1967), esp. pp. 209–210, foreshadowed in his earlier lectures, *Christ the Center* (New York: Harper and Row, 1966).

24. Bonhoeffer, *Letters and Papers from Prison*, p. 197.

25. The theme is developed in *ibid.*, pp. 196–7.

26. Dorothy Sayers, *Four Sacred Plays* (London: Gollancz, 1948), p. 227. Reprinted by permission.

27. Soren Kierkegaard, *Philosophical Fragments* (Princeton: Princeton University Press, 1962), p. 40.

HUMAN AUTONOMY AND
THE PRESENCE OF GOD

Henri Bouillard, S.J.

WE MIGHT BEGIN OUR DISCUSSION of the problem of human autonomy with a statement by Dietrich Bonhoeffer from his well known *Letters and Papers from Prison.*

The movement, beginning about the thirteenth century, . . . towards the autonomy of man (under which head I place the discovery of the laws by which the world lives and deals with itself in science, social and political affairs, art, ethics and religion), has in our time reached a certain completion. Man has learned to cope with all questions of importance without recourse to God as a working hypothesis. . . . As in the scientific field, so in human affairs generally, what we call "God" is being more and more edged out of life, losing more and more ground.[1]

With Bonhoeffer, then, we shall understand human autonomy to mean the autonomy of the world of man and the autonomy of the works of man. This autonomy consists in the fact that social and political organization, civilization, technology, science, ethics, and philosophy, function each according to its own norm, outside the control either of faith or of the Church. Moreover, each of these fields of human activity possesses its

This chapter was translated from the French by Robert E. Donovan.

own meaning and value independent of any reference to a religious origin or end. By means of the free exercise of his reason as well as by his mastery over nature, man has become the agent of his own history. He alone defines the norm, the meaning and the value of his work. To the long process which has led him to this autonomy we give today the name secularization.

For a Christian who believes in the presence of God in the world and who wishes to live in a relationship to that presence, there is the problem of deciding whether he can frankly accept this autonomy and secularization, and the further problem of deciding, once he has accepted it, how he can still be open to the presence of God.

The sphere of human activity where this problem looms largest is that of ethics. For it is above all in this sphere of human existence, that the Christian faith comes face to face with the world of secular culture and civilization. This is so, on the one hand, because no civilization worthy of the name can be conceived without an ethic, and, on the other, because there is no living Christian faith without the gospel ethic. The confrontation is thus both inevitable and decisive.

From this confrontation there arises for us today two symmetrical questions, depending on whether one starts from faith or from one's existence in the world. On the one hand, the Christian wonders under what conditions the gospel ethic taught by the Church can respect human autonomy in a secularized world. On the other hand, while feeling an affinity with unbelievers, the Christian wonders conversely whether ethical existence, the relation of man with man in the world, is a place where human autonomy can be opened to the presence of God. We shall examine each of these questions in turn.

I *The Gospel Ethic and Autonomy*

To begin, let us state precisely the meaning we give to ethics. If we were to say that it consists in the observance of the commandments of God or in the observance of what one must do to merit eternal life, this definition would appear completely insufficient even to a Christian. For it would imply that

130

ethics does not have any meaning for an unbeliever and that, for the believer, it contains no meaning or value of its own, independent of religion. But we know that this is not so. If human conscience admits that it is wrong to kill or to steal, this is not simply because this prohibition is found in the Decalogue; it is rather because human co-existence would be impossible if we would permit ourselves to do to another that which we would not want done to ourselves. In brief, ethics possesses a human significance. It is from the point of view of man that it must be initially defined.

Moral life or morality, in the formal meaning of the term, is the action a reasonable individual performs on himself in order to assure the predominance in him of reason over passion, of the universal over the particular. This implies that the individual can distinguish, in his empirical aims, that which is licit and that which is not, that which is permitted and that which is forbidden. The fundamental category of morality is "duty," and its end is the reasonable happiness of the individual in communion with other individuals. Its fundamental law is respect for humanity, in one's self and in others. No one must ever think of a human being as an object to be used, as a means to an end, but one must treat him always as an end in himself, as a free and reasonable being. But this rule, whose negative thrust is absolute, does not tell us what we must do positively. By itself, it would allow the individual to fall back upon the clarity of its maxim. To become active and efficacious, morality must become action in and upon the world. It must apply itself to the progressive realization of the "kingdom of ends" in the world. It becomes, then, a concrete ethic.[2]

This ethic is determined by the system of multiple relations man enjoys both with nature and his fellow man, according to the different fields of human activity and social life. That which it enunciates as theory, that which it realizes in practice, is the inherent meaning of these diverse relations, that is to say, their essence and the values which they promote. From uncultivated nature and social facts, ethics draws out human meanings and values that man can love. It expresses the logic of freedom insofar as freedom is being-with-another-in-the-world. Its fundamental principle is the recognition given by man to man. Having the positive promotion of meaning as its end, ethics is by that very fact autonomous. It grows out of the freedom which seeks to fulfill itself by introducing into its aims a coherence which their realization verifies. Ethics begins in and for the sake of our world.

Such is the nature of a secular ethics which directs and must direct culture and civilization. Christian morality, on the contrary, which is inspired by the Gospel, seems to come from the outside and to look to the outside. It seems to be affected by a triple exteriority, a triple heteronomy. In the first place it is presented under the mantle of the divine commandments. Secondly, its orientation is eschatological. Finally, the Church attributes to itself the power of defining it and of making its applications precise. The question to be asked, then, is whether or not this Christian ethic can be called ethics in the sense that we understand that term today. Does it give the proper meaning to our world and to our life?

We will turn our attention first to the idea of divine commandment. In archaic societies and in the civilizations of antiquity, the customs which guide the life of men are always thought of as manifesting the sacred order of the world. These customs are based on a collection of myths which relate this order of life to a divine activity occurring in some primordial time. Although these customs are referred to a sacred origin to give them an absolute character, they are nonetheless the same customs inherent in society, customs recognized universally as the expression of an abiding truth about human existence. This is continued, in an analogous fashion, in the Old Testament. There the idea of the divine is, of course, entirely different. In place of a sacral which is different and of manifold gods hardly distinguishable from the world, we find the unique God, creator of a world distinct from himself and active agent intervening in the history of man. The law which this God founds is not different from the ethic which issued from the life and conscience of his people. That the Mosaic law is divinely revealed [3] does not prevent its being the work of a great legislator who corrected and codified the customs of his community. The important biblical scene of Sinai must not be interpreted according to the grotesque imagery presented by the film, *The Ten Commandments,* where one sees lightning flash from the clouds like a welder's arc engraving the divine law on bronze plaques. Centuries ago the Fathers of the Church and the monks of the Middle Ages explained that the images of the Bible need not be understood literally, but should be interpreted as symbols of spiritual realities. What Israel accepted as divine law was the law that her leaders, prophets and scribes had progressively conceived and had put forth with the help of the divine light furnished them. It is the law which the prophets wished to see become more and more interior and which St. Paul will connect with the interior action of the Holy Spirit. Thus, when Christ puts emphasis on the divine command to love our neighbor, it should not be seen as an exterior order that he imposes from outside but as an indication of what each of us should desire to experience from a relationship with our fellow man.

The idea of a divine commandment, then, does not destroy the autonomy of ethics. When the Bible or Christian teaching tells us that God commands this or that, we must not forget that this language is analogous or symbolic. What is signified transcends the mode of signification. God does not command from without as man does, but from the depth of our being-in-the-world, by the very fact that He is its Creator. Strictly speaking, He does not command; rather He grounds what we call commandment, that is to say, the need for meaning and coherence at the heart of human behavior. This need is conceived and formulated by man and it is also man who understands that it is grounded in God.

Let us now consider the particular orientation that the Christian faith gives to ethics. The moral exhortations of the New Testament are governed by the idea of eschatology, that is to say, the concept of the Kingdom of God manifested in Jesus Christ and yet awaiting its final manifestation at the end of time. It is this idea which provides a key to the proper understanding of the Beatitudes and of the Sermon on the Mount. In the Gospels, and especially in the fourth, this eschatological dimension adds vitality to the precept of charity. According to St. Paul, the Christian life is a participation in the death and resurrection of Christ, while we await His return. Christian ethics serves to give life to this faith and hope. It receives its inspiration from them. It is normal, nevertheless, to ask if this ethic can still remain an autonomous ethic, capable of organizing an intelligible human existence in the midst of this world. The answer to this question depends on the meaning one gives to Christian ethics. History shows that an orientation towards the "other worldly" more or less deters certain men from accomplishing tasks in this world, or makes them more attentive to the fear of damnation than to the positive value of the good, or is exploited in certain cases to excuse misery and established disorder. History also shows, however, that this same orientation has acted as a fulcrum allowing men to lift themselves above their inherent selfishness and to participate in selfless activities. It depends on us whether it has the one or the other effect.

A very simple observation will permit us to understand how the Christian ethic retains in principle a "this worldly" value. All that is required is a distinction between *inspiration* and *determination*. The gospel ethic is *inspired* by the love of God and the expectation of His Kingdom already inaugurated in this world by Christ. This inspiration enables the believer to perform actions that he would not be able to perform without it. The *determination* of this ethic, however, in regard to its internal structure, has another origin. The rules of conduct formulated in the New Testament concerning the relationships between men express, in fact, the inherent human structure of these relationships. They take into account certain virtues of pagan morality. The Fathers of the Church and theologians were not, then, unfaithful to the Gospel when they borrowed from pagan philosophers the means of giving a more precise determination to the Christian ethic. In the total course of her life, the Church has integrated into her moral teaching the new values which surfaced in the conscience of humanity.

It is true, however, that, before accepting these values the Church occasionally opposed them for quite a long time. This brings us to a consideration of our third difficulty and leads us into a very sensitive area. As trustee of the gospel message, which implies the responsibility of transmitting and interpreting it, the Church sees itself as having the right and duty of formulating definitions and of giving direction not only in matters of faith but also in the moral sphere. When the Church regulates the religious practices of the faithful, when she steps in to remind them of the meaning of the perfection called for in the Gospels, the questions arising from such action directly concern only the Christian community. When, on the other hand, the Church proposes moral teaching in the strict sense, she intends her words to have a more far-reaching effect, since she claims to be concerned with man in general. If on these occasions she limits herself to a simple reminder of the great principles of justice and love of neighbor, there is no problem. But she frequently goes on to draw up more precise mandates and directives directly concerned with the various fields of human activity: the political, the economic, the organization of society, marriage and family life. In doing this the Church sets herself up as the authentic interpreter not only of the gospel message, but also of that which is called the "natural law." In other words, the Church sees herself as capable of appraising the true meaning of human conduct and being able to judge the ethical value of various human activities. This brings us to a crucial point in our discussion. In regard to the aforementioned directives of the Church, there will always be some men who will approve and welcome them joyfully, as well as some who will resist angrily. But the essential question to be asked is one of principle: can the intervention of the Church respect the autonomous morality of a secular world which considers itself come of age?

Such respect is not inevitably guaranteed. The infallibility promised to the Church assures her essential fidelity to the gospel message and the correctness of her solemn definitions, but it does not insure the perfection of each of her judgments. It has happened in the past that the resistance of the Church to certain new ideas or values was rooted less in an attachment to the gospel message than in an attachment, an all too human attachment, to a certain outdated cultural style or to a social order no longer valid. The Second Vatican Council has had the good sense to recognize this. There the Church has admitted most firmly that in order for her to shed her light on the things of this world, she must first listen to the world and its present aspirations. What is implied in this?

First of all, the natural law whose interpreter the Church claims to be, must be understood in an accurate way. The norm of morality for human existence cannot simply be equated with the order of the cosmos; nor can it be equated with the biological laws common to men and animals. The natural moral law can only be an anthropological law. It stems from an understanding of the meaning of man and of his interpersonal relationships. This law, of course, takes the biological sphere into account, but it relates it to the fulfillment of man. Consequently one cannot dictate anything in the name of the natural law which cannot be justified as an expression of man's well being.

Secondly, since man should be visualized concretely as man-in-history, his mode of existence changing with a change in time and place, the delineation of the "natural law" is subject to certain variations. One cannot, then, conceive this law as a type of legal code which has been uniformly inscribed on the heart of man, as a listing of rules which each man discovers already programmed in him, when he comes to the age of reason. Rather this moral law is reason itself, understood as the power of discerning the meaning of human behavior in the midst of various situations, or, if you will, it is this very meaning, which man discovers more or less clearly, beginning from this or that concrete situation and within the limits of his historical conditioning.

Since the natural moral law is the meaning discovered by reason, by moral conscience, each statement which attempts to express it concretely must be submitted to the critical judgment of men who want to be reasonable and moral; it must be susceptible of recognition by them. Consequently when the Church speaks in the name of the natural law, she involves herself, by this very fact, in a dialogue with men. She can no longer fail to take seriously the moral awareness of those she addresses. While calling herself the guardian of the natural law, the Church must not forget that she is not its unique source. She cannot fulfill her mission without listening to men and without aiming at an agreement with their reasonable proposals. This is why it is fortunate that ecclesiastical authority on all levels has undertaken systematic consultation with the laity, and even with unbelievers, before formulating directives concerning the political, economic, social or marital life of man. Thus she takes the means of effectively respecting the moral autonomy of man and the proper meaning of various human activities.[4] Christian faith and the secular world should therefore be able to meet with sufficient ease on the plane of a common ethic. Neither the idea of a divine commandment, nor the eschatological orientation, nor the intervention of the Church should obstruct, in principle, the autonomy of man discovering and realizing for himself the meaning of his earthly activities. The Christian can be as fully present to the world as other men.

II *Ethical Existence and the Presence of God*

This conclusion now raises a new problem. Does the divine commandment and the eschatological orientation properly interpreted have another function beside that of indicating our need to apply ourselves to this earthly life? Does the Church have another mission apart from representing the ethical conscience of the world? Does not the Christian message, once submitted to the modern hermeneutic, summon us to something besides an efficacious love of men, that is to say, to the transformation of the world with a view towards the full recognition which man must give to man? Is it not fitting to divert our attention from a God who reigns in heaven and direct it towards bringing about the divine immanence in the world? Here is the question which haunts most Christians today, the temptation which awaits almost all of us. This temptation finds a favorable atmosphere, of course, in man's natural tendency to enjoy a more comfortable world and in his legitimate desire of participating unreservedly in research. But I think we can be more precise about the nature of the various influences which have contributed to this atmosphere.

Let us consider, first of all, the thought of Hegel and the movement which issued from the thought of Marx. In the Preface to Hegel's *Phenomenology of Mind*, we read the following impressive although one-sided description of the medieval world:

Time was when man had a heaven decked and fitted out with an endless wealth of thought and pictures. The meaning of anything whatever was to be found in the thread of light by which it was linked to heaven; rather than linger in a mundane presence, the gaze moved beyond, to the divine essence, to a presence, so to say, beyond what we experience here below.[5]

Certainly Hegel is not satisfied with the culture which came after this *Weltanschauung*. He appreciates neither the platitudes of the Enlightenment nor the shallow feeling for the divine which animates romanticism and pietism. He wishes to re-establish the truth of Christianity, this time understood philosophically. According to the well known statement of the *Encyclopedia*, the divine no longer resides in a Church separated from the world and glorifying monastic life. The divine Spirit has penetrated in an immanent manner to the depth of the profane world. Its concrete interiority reveals itself in the institutions of social ethics: marriage, work and above all the State, in which the rationality and freedom of spirit is incarnated.[6] The divine is no longer the Wholly-Other. Marx goes even further in the direction of pure immanence. Having opted for atheism and historical materialism, he jettisons all reference to absolute Spirit and trusts in the revolutionary practice of transforming economic and social conditions. The historical mission of the proletariat is to establish a classless society which will bring about that recognition which man must give to man.

Even outside the communist and progressive sphere, the thought of Marx and that of Hegel have had, at least in Europe and especially since the last war, a considerable influence. They have surely helped make certain Christians more attentive to

138

the needs of this world, to social justice and to the necessity of reform. But one can ask whether these influences have not conditioned man to be almost exclusively interested in worldly occupations to the detriment of developing his religious sense. Why does it happen, for example, that many of Teilhard de Chardin's admirers only emphasize one aspect of his thought, namely his love of the earth, while they fail to point out that this love is unfailingly fused in his thought with a mystical drive toward the God revealed in Jesus Christ? Why does it happen that many preachers are more at ease when they are speaking of giving aid to the underdeveloped nations than when they are calling to mind the mystery of man in his relationship to God?

The mutilation of the gospel message is equally favored by contemporary attempts to elaborate a demythologized Christianity or a secular, non-religious Christianity. Originating in a Protestant milieu, these attempts are finding a sympathetic hearing among Catholics. We must guard against misconstruing the noble motives of the promoters of this new view and the profit that we can reap from their honest work. A Bultmann or a Bonhoeffer are men deeply attached to the Word of God and desirous of making it more accessible to the man of today. But one tends too often to be attracted more by the critical part of their work than by its positive aspects, and certain disciples have pushed its negative aspects to the extreme. The acute sense of divine transcendence which vitalizes the faith of Bultmann, as well as the profoundly Christian life of Bonhoeffer, disappears in the thought of these disciples.

A proper understanding of Bonhoeffer is of special interest to us here. He was a pastor and a theologian who devoted the most important part of his short life to replenishing the meaning of the Church, the communion of saints, the transcendence of the Kingdom of God, and life led in imitation of Christ. He himself led this life in a quasi-monastic way. But for many men, who put all that aside, there remains, in general, only a few pages from his *Letters and Papers from Prison*, in which one finds the groping and indecisive investigation into a non-religious interpretation of biblical concepts. Indeed, serious

139

commentators must admit that it is difficult to define exactly what he means by religion. It would seem that he had above all the pietistic conception in mind, which concentrates all of man's efforts on his interior life and the concern for personal salvation, which causes him to misconstrue earthly realities and view God as a sort of "Stop-gap" which makes up for the deficiencies in our understanding and action. A non-religious Christianity, then, should be a non-pietistic Christianity. This does not mean, however, a Christianity without piety, since throughout his letters Bonhoeffer insists that prayer is his unique refuge and that he regrets the impossibility of celebrating the Lord's Supper as he would have wished. People often neglect to mention this. His imprecise idea of a non-religious Christianity has been seized upon by many thinkers both in Europe and America, and has been given a meaning which probably would have surprised him. There is no need to mention here the well known works of J. A. T. Robinson, Harvey Cox or the so-called "death of God" theologians. They have received excessive publicity. But, as Robinson himself has noted with a touch of humor: the success of a book as of all merchandise depends less on the quality of the product than on the state of the market.

It is precisely this state of the market that interests us. The various ideas that I have just mentioned, some important, others mediocre, all attest by their existence and success to the reality of a problem which is our problem. They invite us to search for God in this world, among men, and not in some hidden world in heaven. While we may feel the truth and importance of such an outlook we also have the feeling that it involves a diminution of man and of the gospel message. I wish to show, therefore, through a reconsideration of some traditional themes, in what sense the presence of God is at the same time immanent and transcendent in the world and in man.

No one of us has invented the affirmation of God; we have discovered it in our culture and above all in the faith of the Church. But to understand what this affirmation means, we must perceive how it is justified. Contemporary thought has familiarized us with an idea as ancient as human reflection, that of our contingency and our finitude. We *are* freedom in the world. But we have not created the world which contributes to our being; we have not created our being; we have not created the freedom which we are. All this has been given to us and continues to be given to us at every moment. All this is given to us only for a time, however, because we cannot overcome death. Our finite freedom, our being-in-the-world, is not its own principle, its own source, its own ground. All that we are, all that we do, the whole system of our relationships with the world and with others, the emergence of our free self amidst these relationships, the possibility of finding there the fulfillment of our being, all this finds its source and ground in an Other than ourselves. Even the idea that we have of this Other comes from him; it expresses his taking possession of our mind. That is why it is self-affirmative.

But this Other, whom we call God, is not a being among other beings. He is neither a planet to be discovered nor a great old man seated on the pinnacle of the skies. Because He is the source of all that is, He is none of the things which are. Inasmuch as He is the "ocean and abyss of being," He is not an "object" which is separated from the world around us and from the knowing subject. As St. Thomas has expressed it, He is outside the order of beings, since He is the principle which penetrates all. According to the strong statement of Nicholas of Cusa, He is the non-other, the *non aliud*. But if He can exist as the non-other, surpassing all intra-worldly otherness, it is because He is the Wholly-Other, the Absolute above all relativity.[7] And if we can perceive Him and relate Him to ourselves despite His inaccessibility, it is because He is immanent in all beings, and especially in our own, as their intimate source and radical ground. If He stands over against us, it is through the world and through ourselves. He appears to us transcendent only through His grounding immanence.

These classic but often forgotten propositions permit us to accept a considerable number of the contemporary ideas just mentioned. We may say with this or that theologian that God is the ground of our being, on condition that we understand by it not the profundity that we can explore but the profundity inaccessible to our view, the place where we emerge out of the Otherness which is our ground. We can equally agree with Bonhoeffer when he says that it is at the heart of our life that God is transcendent, and that the transcendent is not the infinitely distant but the very close. With many current theologians we can emphasize that one finds God in the world, among men, in loving our brothers not only in a few charitable gestures but in the organization of a social life more favorable to the further development of mankind. How could love of neighbor be a test of our love of God unless God be immanent in our neighbor? How could the songs of love gathered together in the Canticle of Canticles be able to symbolize the love of God for man unless there be something holy in the love of a man for a woman? We should have, therefore, no difficulty in recognizing with Hegel that the divine is immanent in social relationships, in marriage, in the working community, in the just State. God is not a presence that we could discover outside of our intra-worldly relationships. He is not an object alongside others, which we could reach by subtracting the others. We cannot love Him in opposition to creation but only through it and in it.

We must now ask a further question, namely whether our love of God is in fact nothing else but our love for man and our diligence in earthly affairs. The presence of God to the world and to ourselves is a silent presence, a hidden presence that we can easily misunderstand, forget or ignore. This must be as it is, to insure the autonomy of our being-in-the-world and of our activity, and to make the world open to our freedom. When we fathom the depths of nature by scientific studies, when we become masters of it through technology, we proceed and must proceed as if God did not exist, *etsi deus non daretur*, according to the expression of Bonhoeffer. We cannot appeal to Him to close the gaps in our knowledge or in our technology. The same is true for the economic and political structure of society. One must achieve this organization according to the proper sense and internal structure of each relationship. Seen in this way, economics, politics, as well as technology and science are atheistic. They are atheistic not

142

because they would deny God, but because, on the one hand, this is not the place to introduce God as one factor among many, and, on the other, because a political structure must exercise its authority over believers and unbelievers alike.

Will this necessary neglect of God prove definitive? No, for if it is true that God is the source of our being, of our activity, and the ground of all meaning, we cannot fulfill ourselves, in our own truth, without recognizing His grounding presence. Moreover, the real conditions of human co-existence bid us open ourselves to a reconciling presence. Each of us has his dream of a coherent and meaningful social existence and we want to work for its realization. Yet it is difficult to fail to recognize that in each sphere of social life an internal contradiction appears which admits of no complete resolution. The sexual union between man and woman, which is immediately the language of desire, must become, if it is to be truly human, the language of love. Yet between "desire" which wishes to possess for its own sake and "love" which wishes the good of the other, there is a sort of antinomy which can be resolved only partially, in adjustments which are always unstable. In economic society, where work is constitutive, the complexity of trade and the desire for gain lead to disorders and injustices that even a non-capitalistic system cannot entirely repair. In political life, the will to power stirs up within nations and among nations constantly recurring struggles. These various contradictions inherent within social life are the sign of an irreducible and tragic otherness, which forces us either to violate the other or to struggle against ourselves for another's respect.

Certainly the other than ourselves does not simply serve as our limit. It is primarily that without which we could not live nor be ourselves. Throughout our existence we have need of the other not only as an instrument at our disposal, but also as an *alter ego* which gives us recognition and receives it from us. The tragedy is that this recognition, this respect for personal otherness, burdens us with renunciations and sacrifices which seem to assume, in the context of our fragile and mortal life, the appearance of absolute loss. The tragedy is that this recognition should so often be broken by a denial of the required renunciations.

This existential contradiction attests at the same time to the radical finitude of man in the world and to his fallibility. This very fact challenges us somehow to go beyond the horizon of this world, or, more precisely, to search throughout the world for the presence of a Wholly-Other who, by absolving it, would justify it.

Thus by reflecting on ethical existence, on the relationship of man with man, we are challenged to take into consideration, as the means of a possible hope, the Christian message, the idea of a God who, within history and in the person of Jesus Christ, has reconciled the world to Himself. To the extent that the ocean and abyss of being, the ontological mystery which grounds our existence and our relationships, takes on for us the guise of someone who loves us and whom we can love, and who opens for us the hope of an absolute future in Him; to that extent we should be able by His love to transfigure our love for men and be able to anticipate, in faith, an end to the existential contradiction which introduces a tragic element into otherness, we should be able, then, to give a sure meaning to this confusion of fleeting joys and lasting distress, of darkness and illumination, which constitutes our co-existence with men. We should be able to believe in a final hope which enlightens human history, that mish-mash production of splendor and mediocrity, where the cunning of reason often uses cruelty and violence, where the highest realizations of culture have frequently been built on the misery of men.

It is precisely this hope which faith in Christ supplies. Following Bonhoeffer, people today like to present Jesus as "the man for others," the one who lived and died for others. Faith in Him consists in participating in this being-for-others, in devoting oneself to suffering humanity. In this lies the experience of transcendence. There is in this an essential truth, which will, however, lose its force if one forgets that in Jesus it is God who is man for others. Fear of a simplistic objectivization should not force us to suppress the mystery of the divine presence. Theological reflection permits us to understand that

144

one can, without abandoning oneself to mythology, acknowledge in the existence of Jesus the "ex-sistence" of God in this world, His epiphany in human history.[8] The same is true of the resurrection of Christ. Some people tell us today that the return to the life of this world of a dead body is for modern man unthinkable. This is exactly the same reaction of the Athenians who were listening to Paul on the Areopagus. But it is clear from the New Testament that the resurrection of Jesus was not a return to the life of this world. St. Thomas has clearly explained this by specifying that the life of the resurrected Christ is an immortal life, a life allied with that of God, a mysterious life which transcends ordinary understanding and which was only grasped by the Apostles in faith.[9] It is this life which removes the scandal of the cross, allowing us to see in it the love of God for men, and it is this life which serves as the ground of our hope in an absolute future.

This hope should not turn us away from the earth nor from man, since it actually summons us to recognize in them a meaning and a value, even when meaning and value seem to be lacking. To love the earth and to love men in God and in the hope of an absolute future is not to stop loving them in and for themselves. For, to repeat, God is immanent in the creation which He grounds. And the redemption, far from disabling creation, leads it towards its end. The transcendence of the Kingdom of God recalls us to the proper meaning of our undertakings and of human co-existence.

Let me conclude this presentation by summing it up in a few statements. Ethics unfolds the meaning of interpersonal relationships; it is autonomous, and the divine is immanent within it. But the irreducible otherness of the other, his distress which calls upon our justice and love, the tragedy of violence and sacrifice, recalls us to a Wholly-Other, which is the absolute future of our co-existence. Because this Wholly-Other is the source and ground of our freedom and of our being-with-another-in-the-world, He is at the same time the non-other. Religious faith, through which we open ourselves to His revelatory and reconciling action, emerges amidst interpersonal relationships. It is in the depth of the present life that

145

Christian faith gives further meaning to these relationships, in anticipation of that meaning they shall have in their fulfillment.

NOTES

1. Letter of June 8, 1944, in Dietrich Bonhoeffer, *Letters and Papers from Prison* (New York: Macmillan, 1967), pp. 167–168.
2. See E. Weil, *Philosophie politique* (Paris: Vrin, 1956, première partie); *Philosophie morale* (Paris: Vrin, 1961).
3. The primary constitutive element in divine revelation is in fact God's promises to His people. In relation to these promises the Mosaic law is secondary. But we cannot retrace here the various stages of their progressive elaboration.
4. See P. Antoine, "Conscience et loi naturelle," *Etudes*, 313 (1963), pp. 162–183.
5. G. W. F. Hegel, *Phänomenologie des Geistes* (Hamburg: Meiner, 1948), p. 14.
6. G. W. F. Hegel, *Encyclopädie* (Leipzig: Meiner, 1949), pp. 458–459.
7. See H. Urs von Balthasar, *Dieu et l'homme d'aujourd'hui* (Paris: Desclee de Brouwer, 1958), p. 182, p. 255.
8. See Karl Rahner, "Current Problems in Christology," *Theological Investigations*, Vol. I (Baltimore: Helicon, 1961).
9. *Summa Theologica*, pars III, ques. 55, art. 2 and 4.

been a major factor in the unsettling of every concordat between theology and a particular philosophy.

Dr. Hendrick Kraemer, writing on the relation between Christianity and the broad phenomenon of religion, has a description of one famous alliance between theology and philosophy. Referring to a particular thinker, he says the following:

He has produced a system which is a marvel of balance and equilibrium, in which classical rationalism, Christian dogma, and mysticism are splendidly combined. It is a feast for the intellectual connoisseur, but its balance is artificial and falsifies the true perspective of the biblical revelation, being obtained at the cost of distorting and obscuring the biblical Christian faith.[2]

Once when I was giving a lecture on Paul Tillich I played a harmless trick on my students by reading that passage as though it were a criticism of Tillich, revealing to them only later that Dr. Kraemer wrote those words about Thomas Aquinas. They seemed to me to apply formally to Tillich also as Tillich is often understood. I am sure that in both cases there is always the possibility of appealing to the real St. Thomas or to the real Paul Tillich and to find that both thinkers transcended this theological portrayal. Yet today those who share the tendency to resist absolutistic and static concepts of the divine nature would often find a similar problem in both of these thinkers, however different they were in the substance of their thought. Tillich did make room for the more dynamic theological ideas, but by the time they were absorbed into his system they seemed to be very much tamed. Verbally he was able to unite such categories as freedom and destiny, or being and non-being, and he was also able to include the attributes of God that were suggested both by his ontological system and by the biblical symbols, but the relationship between them always remained precarious. I am impressed by the utter honesty with which he faced this precarious relationship between the biblical and the ontological elements in his thought in his little book, *Biblical Religion and the Search for Ultimate Reality*. The next to the last paragraph of that book has never seemed to me to receive as much attention as it deserves. Tillich, after spending so many years in fashioning his own synthesis of theology and ontology or metaphysics, in that passage seems to me to throw the door wide open for new experiments. He says:

The correlation of ontology and biblical religion is an infinite task. There is no special ontology which we have to accept in the name of the biblical message, neither that of Plato nor that of Aristotle, neither that of Cusanus nor that of Spinoza, neither that of Kant nor that of Hegel, neither that of Lao-tze nor that of Whitehead. There is no saving ontology, but the ontological question is a necessary task. *Against* Pascal I say: The God of Abraham, Isaac, and Jacob and the God of the philosophers is the same God. He is a person and the negation of himself as a person.[3]

Tillich opened the door to various philosophical experiments. In that last sentence did he close it again? I am not sure, and I leave the question for others to answer who know more about Tillich. But in the earlier sentences he did show us a way beyond St. Thomas and even beyond himself. He represented the uneasiness which Protestant theology has usually felt in the presence of each particular system of philosophy, when it tends to become dominant.

Does the absence of any close Protestant alliance of theology and philosophy cause Protestants to be more at sea than Roman Catholics in the present situation? I am not sure about the answer to that question. It does mean that Protestants have less to rebel against when they assume the role of rebel. The classical ontological or metaphysical concepts have never had as strong a hold on the minds of the Protestant as has been the case with Catholic theologians in the modern period. There are fewer barriers to the influence of the existentialist, the dynamic, and in the broadest sense of the word, the personalistic, concepts that are natural to biblical thought. And yet there is another side to this. I can illustrate it with reference to the radical theologians who have no place for any conception of the transcendence of God and yet who are Christo-centric. Though in some respects, to which I shall refer later, I have been helped by Barth's presentation of the nature of God, I believe that the Barthian rejection of all preparation for belief in God apart from the receiving of revelation has made it natural for some of his followers to lose faith in God even though they retain faith in Christ, strange as this may seem.

The rejection of the rationalistic natural theology that confidently speaks of proofs of God, is in my judgment correct. But I do not believe that we should reject all preparation for faith in God that may be given in "general revelation," or in the kind of questioning concerning the human condition which does not depend on Christion revelation, questioning of the kind characteristic of Paul Tillich's very helpful method of correlation. Similar to this is what John Macquarrie calls a descriptive natural theology. These are intimations of God, not proofs of God, in the human condition, including man's aspirations and thought which have marks of remarkable self-transcendence, as well as his absolute dependence as a creature threatened with nothingness. To reject all preparations for and confirmations of faith in God which have meaning to people who know nothing of the biblical revelation, is to prepare the way for atheism. To do this is a kind of theological purism that is quite unnecessary and which cuts us off from many aspects of reality, even from real questions.

I think that this narrowing of the base of belief in God is greatest in those who even leave aside the Old Testament revelation as bringing its own witness. To reduce Christian faith to the movement of the New Testament *kerygma*, to the cross followed by the resurrection, and to treat the Old Testament as having no significance in itself but only as the first volume of a Christian book, is to deny to the Church a very important support for its faith. When all things come down to a single point, faith is more precarious than when that point is supported by the whole history of response of men to the God of Abraham, Isaac and Jacob, the God of the psalmists and prophets. Do we not have here a line rather than a point? This earlier revelation is fulfilled for the Christian by the revelation in Christ but not displaced by it. It has great meaning for faithful Jews who do not regard Christ as normative.

I realized the importance of this when I discovered that the writings of Abraham Heschel made most helpful and fresh devotional reading. Is there not a preparatory *kerygma* before the New Testament in such words as these from Isaiah:

For thus says the high and lofty one who inhabits eternity, whose name is Holy: I dwell in the high and holy place and also with him who is of a contrite and humble spirit, to revive the spirit of the humble and the heart of the contrite.[4]

Is it not possible that this broader apprehension of God in the Old Testament may make contact with more varied aspects of experience than the New Testament proclamation itself? It is no source of proofs, but it may provide pointers as well as express anticipatory experiences, confirmations, even corrections, of a Christianity based upon a single event.

One thing that impresses me about the history of the relationship between philosophy and the substance of Christian faith is that the latter has survived so many philosophies. I think that while it is difficult to put into a formula what this substance is, it has its own authority as Christians respond to it in each situation. We today respond to it as we find it in the biblical record; we do so while we also respond to the responses of our predecessors (in other words, to tradition). What comes to us in this process as the central biblical message we must continually relate to philosophy, but this will take place amidst free discussion between various philosophical options and various biblical interpretations. This is a never-ending process. At no point can either the apprehension of the center of the biblical message or the tradition or the philosophy be frozen. All of this does not give us a neat package, but neat packages of thought have a way of becoming unwrapped.

I believe that the current rebellion against traditional Christian theism is based in part on misunderstandings of the biblical teaching about God. I shall deal with three misunderstandings which keep reappearing in the discussion of God that one hears today.

First is the assumption that faith in God and worship of God are a great diversion from service to man, that God competes with the neighbor for our attention. As is the case with all three misunderstandings that I shall mention, the Churches have often acted as though the view of God rejected were the correct one. The life of piety has often led one away from involvement in the world of neighbors with their secular problems. Preoccupation with the internal development of theology, important as that is in its place, can also have this effect. Wonder and gratitude, repentance and commitment which become worship, should not be seen as extra duty to God that competes with our duties to our neighbors. Indeed God as we know Him in the biblical revelation goes out in aggressive love to those same neighbors. Ultimately God should be worshipped for His own sake but the very logic of Christian worship turns us to the creatures whom God loves.

The prophets of Israel were as critical of religion as an escape from social responsibility as any of the modern critics. "Bring no more vain offerings, incense is an abomination to me," says the opening chapter of Isaiah. "Cease to do evil, learn to do good, seek justice, correct oppression, defend the fatherless, plead for the widow." [5] The New Testament is equally clear that commitment to God is not in competition with commitment to the welfare and dignity of the neighbor, of all neighbors. This is true of John and Paul and of the Synoptic Gospels. "If anyone says, 'I love God' and hates his brother, he is a liar; for he who does not love his brother whom he has seen, cannot love God whom he has not seen." [6] "So faith, hope, love abide, these three; but the greatest of these is love." [7] I might add that you can hardly interpret "love" in that passage as primarily love for God because when love is described in earlier sentences in this same passage it clearly refers to the human context of love. I refer to such words as "love is patient and kind; love is not jealous or boastful; it is not arrogant or rude." [8] Perhaps the most vivid of all are the words in the story of the last judgment: "Lord, when did we see you hungry or thirsty or a stranger or naked or sick or in prison, and did not minister to you?" And his answer is: "Truly, I say to you, as you did it not to the least of these, you did it not to me." [9]

In principle the issue is clear. The verses that I have quoted

153

are no isolated proof texts. They express the spirit of the New Testament, the spirit of Him about whom the New Testament is written. There is psychological competition in practice between churchly activities and private acts of worship on the one hand, and acts of love and concern for people in the world. This becomes especially difficult when service to neighbors involves political movements and large-scale social action which have their own ambiguities. It is easy to escape from them to acts of personal or churchly piety which are related to the more obvious acts of service to individual neighbors. But the more we realize that the God whom we worship is Himself involved in the events of history, that He loves not only individuals in their spiritual aspect but persons in community and all that concerns their temporal and material welfare, the less should we feel competition between service to God and service to men.

There is a second and probably more deeply felt difficulty created by a misunderstanding of Christian theism. This is the assumption that God in His sovereignty and power overwhelms man, leaving no space for man's freedom or dignity or humanity. This idea keeps reappearing in history. It was an essential factor in the nineteenth-century atheism of Ludwig Feuerbach and of Karl Marx. It is an essential motif in the current Christian ideas that border on atheism. It is expressed in the revolt of most radical theologians against the absolutistic views of God to which I have referred. I hope that, in the dialogue between Christians and Marxists in which Roman Catholics are fortunately taking such leadership, this is one matter on which a real misunderstanding can in time be cleared up. No intellectual clearing-up is sufficient in itself in matters of faith, but it can remove obstacles.

There is no doubt that doctrines of God have been presented in Christian history which theoretically leave no room for human initiative if you press their logic to the bitter end. Yet even doctrines of this sort, as in the case of Calvin's teaching about God's absolute sovereignty leading to the idea of double predestination, did not have the effect of downgrading the dignity of the original Calvinists. They were able to believe that this God whom they worshipped had elected them to be His instruments, that He was on their side. Perhaps their being His instruments and God being their instrument became confused at times. In Protestant history this doctrine inspired a proud, all too self-sufficient individualism, and a sense of the righteous community. There is a whole literature about the relation between Calvinism and the rise and flourishing of capitalistic individualism. When ideas concerning the absolute sovereignty and power of God are received at second hand, are somewhat secularized without the original piety or the original sense of an enabling grace that went with them, they can easily seem to be incompatible with any full sense of the freedom, dignity and humanity of man. The much emphasized semi-Pelagianism attributed to Catholics by Protestants is a protection against this one-sidedness.

However, this one-sided absolutism in the doctrine of God is itself a caricature of the biblical understanding of God. God as we know Him in the Bible does not force His way upon His people. He pleads with Israel in the words of Isaiah: "Why do you spend your money for that which is not bread and your labor for that which does not satisfy? Incline your ear, and come to me. Seek the Lord while he may be found." [10] Earlier the prophet Hosea agonized over the disobedience of Israel: "What shall I do with you, O Ephraim? What shall I do with you, O Judah?" [11] Never far away are, to be sure, the themes of judgment and wrath and punishment, but God pleads with his people to choose the way of obedience. The punishment is a sign that He has failed to win His people for He does not compel them. Man is free to resist God, obedience does not come as the effect of sheer divine power or divine manipulation. God does not offer us today a secure way of avoiding nuclear annihilation. He draws, He persuades, He seeks to win, but He does not compel.

The theme of the weakness of God pervades the scriptures as well as the themes of His sovereignty and His power. The cross of Christ is itself a demonstration of both, but only to faith. Think of the great words in which the Church has seen anticipations of the cross of Christ:

155

Behold my servant, whom I uphold,
My chosen in whom my soul delights:
I have put my spirit upon him—
He will bring forth justice to the nations.

He will not cry or lift up his voice
  or make it heard in the street:
A bruised reed he will not break,
And a dimly burning wick he will not quench;
He will faithful bring forth justice.[12]

There is a direct line for the Christian between these words in Isaiah and the story of Christ, from "like a lamb that is led to the slaughter" to "He saved others; let him save himself." Dietrich Bonhoeffer says: "God allows himself to be edged out of the world, and that is exactly the way, the only way, in which He can be with us and help us." [13] To say that alone is to break the paradox, a paradox that is deeper than theological formulations. Christians tempted by atheism despair of ever again relating God's weakness to His power as is done so pervasively in the Bible. They see God on the cross but have difficulty in seeing Him as the creator of the world and the Lord of history. But both perceptions of God are there in the revelation. God as known in the Old and New Testaments is not a threat to the freedom, dignity and humanity of man. Both His power and His weakness represent problems, but let neither of these problems displace the other.

The third misunderstanding is closely related to the second. It is the assumption that God's absolute control over all that happens in history makes it impossible to believe in Him because of the many monstrous forms of evil that He causes or permits. This is an ancient theme but it has special force at a time when evil is experienced on so vast a scale that it is almost impossible to see it as having positive value in the formation or disciplining of men. This would be especially true of the prospect of nuclear annihilation. But it was also true of the experience of the death camps and other large-scale massacres which have destroyed the persons who might be the means of grace for others in a total catastrophe. The individual in his suffering is supported by others who mediate grace and healing, but what if the whole human community is destroyed or deeply corrupted? This scale of evil fits into none of the usual ways of dealing with the problem of evil when God's control is thought of as unlimited. I find the outcry of Rabbi Richard Rubenstein very natural in his book, *After Auschwitz*, given the absolutistic conception of God that he presupposes. He writes:

I believe the greatest single challenge to modern Judaism arises out of the question of God and the death camps. . . . How can Jews believe in an omnipotent, beneficent God after Auschwitz? Traditional Jewish theology maintains that God is the ultimate, omnipotent actor in the historical drama. It has interpreted every major catastrophe in Jewish history as God's punishment of a sinful Israel. I fail to see how this position can be maintained without regarding Hitler and the SS as instruments of God's will. The agony of European Jewry cannot be likened to the testing of Job. To see any purpose in the death camps, the traditional believer is forced to regard the most demonic, antihuman explosion in all history as a meaningful expression of God's purposes. The idea is simply too obscene for me to accept.[14]

For a time this response led Rabbi Rubenstein to atheism, though in his book he seems to be moving toward a meaningful faith in God in terms that are similar to one aspect of Tillich's thought, namely, to God as the focus of ultimate concern and ground of being, as the central reality against which all partial realities can be measured, and hence as the means of overcoming all idolatries with their various forms of enslavement.

But Rubenstein's problem is in part the result of a one-sided reading of the biblical understanding of God. It does not do justice to the aspects of God's weakness or self-limitations (but why self-limitations at the price of Auschwitz?) which also belong to the biblical view. It is obscene to say that God willed the death camps of Hitler, but it can be seen how in God's world such things can happen as the result of the ripening of evil and its cumulative effects that are the result of man's freedom to resist God. One can say that such evil brings judgment on itself and that in this fact there is a sign of divine providence, a sign of the limits to human evil that belong to the structure of things. I used to say this often, before there appeared the possibility of ending history through the use of nuclear weapons. Now I do not know what to do with that possibility in terms of a theodicy or of any consistent way of dealing with the relation of God to evil. The situation is not made easier theoretically by the fact that the extent of the destruction that can come to humanity through nuclear war is not a sign of greater depravity, but rather of the fact that technology has outrun human control and even what seemed to be the providential limits of evil. The degree of the catastrophe is not matched by an increase in the degree of evil intent. Indeed, nuclear holocaust is likely to come not out of more guilty behavior among men generally, but out of the folly of elites who are sure that they are right and that it is the moral obligation of each camp to deter the other from imposing its style of life on the world. Perhaps the prospect of this final catastrophe may deter them both and force them to find another way. In that case we may still believe in the providential limits of evil. But all through this process, human freedom to resist the purposes of God, to carry on false crusades or to wage holy wars, or merely to be corrupted by the arrogance of power or the illusion of national omnipotence, will be a factor which is not completely under God's control. If that is heresy, then we shall have to make the best of it.

Here I shall bring in a witness not often heard today in the theological discussion in this country. I do not cite him as a defender of the point that I have just made but of a much broader position: the belief that, whatever may be true of God, He does not threaten the freedom, dignity and humanity of man. I refer to Karl Barth, probably the greatest figure in the Protestant world in this century. His words are important because usually he is regarded as the man who taught that God is completely other than man, that God's sovereignty, majesty and power completely swamp the human creature. There were slogans taken from Barth's earlier writings which did have that effect. But in his writings for the last twenty-five years he has moved far away from this. In his great work, *Church Dogmatics*, there is a beautiful section on "the basic form of humanity." His later work, *The Humanity of God*, also gives this side of his thought. The following quotation is typical:

Man is human in the fact that he is with his fellow-man gladly. But in Christianity there is an inveterate tendency to ignore or not to accept this; not to know or not to want to know this reality of humanity. The reason is obvious. . . . It is thought that the grace of God will be magnified if man is represented as a blotted or an empty page. But in the light of grace itself, of the connection between the humanity of Jesus and humanity generally, this representation cannot be sustained. Man cannot be depicted as a blotted or empty page.[15]

This is important because the usual charge against Barth is exactly this, that he depicts man as a blotted or empty page. Barth goes on to say that the Church's idea of man is so distorted because of this tendency that man "will rightly defend himself against what he has been told. He will not be convicted of his sin if he is uncharitably—and falsely—addressed concerning his humanity." [16]

I shall now turn to one issue that underlies most of the contemporary discussion about the nature of God. Is there any real meaning in the idea of God's transcendence? Or are we to think of God as a human ideal, as a spirit in our midst, or in some other way as wholly immanent in history? When I speak of transcendence I refer to the idea that God is prior to man, to the assumption that His being is not dependent on man but that man is dependent on God, that He is objective, over against man, that He is other than man in His righteousness and His love. Now it is not necessary to suggest that He is wholly other, that there is no continuity between the human and the divine. Take as an illustration the familiar passage in Isaiah: "For my thoughts are not your thoughts, neither are your ways my ways, says the Lord. For as the heavens are higher than the earth so are my ways higher than your ways and my thoughts than your thoughts." [17] The context of those words makes it clear that God is other than man, not in some completely alien characteristic that has nothing in common with human experience, but rather in God's capacity to show mercy and to pardon. Mercy and pardoning are not alien to us. We know something of them in our own experience, though according to the biblical view of God, His mercy and His pardoning still remain a surprise. The surprise is quite similar to that which must have been felt by Peter when Jesus said to him that one should forgive "not seven times but seventy times seven."

Often it is suggested that the very idea of the transcendence of God is a metaphysical idea that is meaningless. Consequently I think that it would be useful to call attention to two effects which the idea of transcendence has had on the way in which we see ourselves and the world.

In the first place it can be the ultimate basis for freeing us from captivity to the human thoughts and ways that have most power and authority over us. It can help to liberate us from bondage to ourselves and to the human principalities and the powers that control us. God is not Himself bound by our human absolutes. God brings under question everything in our personal lives, in our culture, our state and our church. God is free to create, judge and redeem, to make all things new beyond all of our human planning, beyond our expectations and our ideals. God is above us in the sense that He is other than ourselves, other than our nations, other than our ideologies, other than our churches. Let us not get entangled in the difficulties which the bishop of Woolwich emphasized when he criticized the image of God as *up there* or *out there*. These spatial metaphors refer to God as other than man. This otherness of God, this freedom of God, may be the ultimate source of our own freedom. The Christian faith is not meant to be the means by which we give religious and moral sanction to what we are inclined to value and support anyway. Rather it is that which enables us to take a fresh look at what we support. This lies behind the tension that is often noticed between the Christian faith and the nation, not only between Christian faith and the obvious evils in our national life, such as racism and crime and corruption and all that is shoddy and trivial, but also between Christian faith and our national idealism, our assumption that we know what is best for people on other continents, that because we have these ideals our overwhelming power as a nation must be beneficent.

The deepest meaning of the separation of Church and state is not contained in our discussion about such matters as the Blaine Amendment or aid to parochial schools, but rather it has to do with the role of the Church, that responds to the revelation of the transcendent God, as a base for citizens who must always live in tension with the claims and pretensions of the nation and the state, the state as the nation's political structure. Indeed at times the words: "we must obey God rather than men" are derivative from the words: "so are my ways higher than your ways and my thoughts than your thoughts."

A second effect of the idea of the transcendence of God is that our ultimate faith does not depend upon the fate of men in this world but upon the outcome of human history. History-centered or man-centered forms of religion, while they are often morally very fruitful and may be corrections of a one-sided theism of the kind to which I have referred, leave us without faith or hope in the face of the end of history. Professor Hans Morgenthau makes an interesting point when he says that the prospect of nuclear war threatens the meaning of life for the secularists. As long as it is possible for one to believe that the human race will long outlast the individual, the positive meaning of life for such a person is not immediately threatened.[18] In the Old Testament the survival of the nation was generally sufficient. Yet this only postpones the problem if human history is to be brought to an end either by a mad act of man or by a cosmic event. How can faith and hope be proof against every human fate unless God Himself is independent of our history? Perhaps such faith and hope are denied us anyway. If that is the case, we must make the best of it.

It is in this eschatological context, this context of ultimate destiny that I find it most difficult to accept an atheistic view of life. In recent years, when I have seen parts of our globe on television screens as pictures have been taken of it from outer space, I have had forced upon me an ultimate question more vividly than ever before. To see our world as an object in this way stirs my imagination when I think of the possibility that it may at some time be uninhabited by conscious beings. Even more than that, what of all that has happened on this planet, the amazing development of systems of cumulative meaning, of cultures, of religions? Whether you take music or mathematics or science or moral aspirations or love or worship, this planet has been the scene of developments that are extraordinary and precious. To be sure, it is also a place where men threaten one another and kill one another and where most of them are hungry and do not have a chance to develop their capacities, but these facts do not cancel all that is positive in history. If history comes to an end will all of this be lost without a trace, will it be forgotten? Will there be no being in existence that even remembers that there was a human race, a Christ? Is human awareness the only awareness of the meaning of it all? It is not a sufficient alternative to say that there may be similar adventures on other planets and that the history of the cosmos will contain other centers of meaning. This will not compensate for the waste of all that has happened here or for its disappearance from awareness. This is not an argument, but rather a statement of alternatives at the point where the differences between them are most fateful and most clear. We have to respond and choose. The choice is a choice of faith rather than the result of argument, but it is a prior choice to the choice of a uniquely Christian position, and I believe that it prepares the way for the kind of response to Christ which becomes the Christian choice.

NOTES

1. William Hamilton, "The Death of God Theology," *The Christian Scholar*, 48 (1965), p. 31.
2. Hendrick Kraemer, *Religion and the Christian Faith* (London: Lutterworth, 1956), p. 164.
3. Paul Tillich, *Biblical Religion and the Search for Ultimate Reality* (Chicago: Univ. of Chicago Press, 1952), p. 85.
4. Isaiah 57:15–16.
5. *Ibid.* 1:17.
6. 1 John 4:20.

7. 1 Corinthians 13:13.
8. *Ibid.* 13:40.
9. Matthew 25:44–45.
10. Isaiah 55:2.
11. Hosea 6:4.
12. Isaiah 42:1–3.
13. Dietrich Bonhoeffer, *Prisoner for God* (New York: Macmillan, 1953), p. 164.
14. Richard L. Rubenstein, *After Auschwitz* (New York: Bobbs-Merrill, 1966), p. 153.
15. Karl Barth, *Church Dogmatics*, Vol. III, Part 2 (Edinburgh: T. & T. Clark, 1960), pp. 278–279.
16. *Ibid.*
17. Isaiah 55:8–9.
18. Hans Morgenthau, "Western Values and Total War," *Commentary*, 32 (1961), p. 281.

THE ABSENCE OF GOD
IN MODERN CULTURE

Bernard J. Lonergan, S.J.

I THINK I SHOULD BEGIN not with modern culture but with its classical predecessor. Even as little as fifty years ago classical culture was still dominant in American Catholic circles. Then it was named simply culture. It was conceived absolutely, as the opposite of barbarism. It was a matter of acquiring and assimilating the tastes and skills, the ideals, virtues and ideas, that were pressed upon one in a good home and through a curriculum in the liberal arts. This notion, of course, had a very ancient lineage. It stemmed out of Greek παιδεία and Roman *doctrinae studium atque humanitatis*, out of the exuberance of the Renaissance and its pruning in the Counter Reformation-schools of the Jesuits. Essentially it was a normative rather than an empirical notion of culture, a matter of models to be imitated, of ideal characters to be emulated, of eternal verities and universally valid laws.

The defect of this notion of culture was, of course, its particularity. It referred not to the cultures of mankind but to a particular culture that may be named classicist. The need to revise this notion was a need to generalize, to discern in the cultures of mankind their common generic function and the differences in the mode in which that function was fulfilled whether among primitive tribes or in the ancient high civilizations or in the nations and states of historical times.

To this end I should like to recall a distinction sometimes made between the social and the cultural.[1] The social is conceived as a way of life, a way in which men live together in some orderly and so, predictable fashion. Such orderliness is to be observed in the family and in manners, in society with its classes and elites, in education, in the state and its laws, in the economy and technology, in the churches and sects. Such is the social and it is upon it that the cultural arises. For men not only do things. They wish to understand their own doing. They wish to discover and to express the appropriateness, the meaning, the significance, the value, the use of their way of life as a whole and in its parts. Such discovery and expression constitute the cultural and, quite evidently, culture stands to social order as soul to body, for any element of social order will be rejected the moment it is widely judged inappropriate, meaningless, irrelevant, useless, just not worth while.

Now if it is granted that culture is the meaning of a way of life, cultures may be divided according to the manner that meaning is apprehended and communicated. On all cultural levels there are rites and symbols, language and art. Their meaning is felt and intuited and acted out. It is like the meaning already in the dream before the therapist interprets it, the meaning of the work of art before the critic focuses on it and relates it to other works, the endlessly nuanced and elusive and intricate meaings of everyday speech, the intersubjective meaning of smiles and frowns, speech and silence, intonation and gesture, the passionate meanings of interpersonal relations, of high deeds and great achievements, of all we admire, praise, revere, adore, and all we dislike, condemn, loathe, abominate. Such is meaning for undifferentiated consciousness, and it would seem to constitute the spontaneous substance of every culture.

Besides undifferentiated, there also is differentiated consciousness. It is not content to act out what it feels and intuits. Rather it seeks to mirror spontaneous living by analyzing it, making all its elements explicit, subjecting them to scrutiny, evaluation, criticism. So art and literature become the affair not only of artists and writers but also of critics and historians. The creations of craftsmen and artisans are supplanted by the discoveries of scientists and the inventions of technologists. The proverbs of wise men give place to the reflections of philosophers. Religions are complicated by theologies. The destinies of persons and peoples not only work themselves out but also are studied by biographers, historians, psychologists, economists, sociologists and political theorists.

Modern culture shares with its classicist predecessor this reflexive, objectifying component. Both suppose ways of human living. Both ways have immanent meanings. In both this immanent meaning is elaborated, expanded, evaluated, justified or rejected in the criticism of art and of letters, in science and philosophy, in history and theology. In both there is the disastrous possibility of a conflict between human living as it can be lived and human living as a cultural superstructure dictates it should be lived.

Beyond similarities there are differences. Of these the most fundamental was the development of the modern notion of science, a development that has been described by Herbert Butterfield as one that "outshines everything since the rise of Christianity and reduces the Renaissance and the Reformation to the rank of mere episodes, mere internal displacements, within the system of medieval Christendom." [2] For, as I should put it, what occurred towards the end of the seventeenth century was the beginning not merely of much more and much better science but, basically, of a notion of science quite different from the notion worked out by Aristotle and taken for granted by his followers. To put the matter summarily, necessity was a key notion for Aristotle but today it is marginal; in its place is verifiable possibility. Causality was a key notion for Aristotle but today in effect, if not in name, it is replaced by correlation. The universal and abstract were normative in Aristotelian science, but modern science uses universals as tools in its unrelenting efforts to approximate to concrete process. Where the Aristotelian claimed certitude, the modern

166

scientist disclaims anything more than probability. Where the Aristotelian wished to know things in their essences and properties, the modern scientist is satisfied with control and results. Finally, the prestige of this new idea of science is unquestioned, its effectiveness has been palpably demonstrated, its continuing necessity for the survival of the earth's teeming population is beyond doubt.

It was inevitable that the success of the new idea of science should profoundly affect the rest of the cultural superstructure, that what worked in the natural sciences should have repercussions in the human sciences, in philosophy, in theology. However, the exact nature and measure of this influence have varied, and it will clarify issues, I think, if major differences are indicated.

The fields to which I referred by speaking of the human sciences are known in America as behavioral sciences and in Germany as *Geisteswissenschaften*. The American name stresses the analogy of natural and human science: in both one observes performance, proposes hypothetical correlations, and endeavors to verify one's hypotheses as probably true. The German name stresses the basic difference between natural and human science. As it was worked out by Wilhelm Dilthey, this difference lies in the very data of the two types. The data for a natural science are just given. One needs language to describe them, classify them, identify them; one needs instruments to observe and measure them; but what counts is not the language, but just what happens to be given to this and any other observer. In the human sciences, on the other hand, there are of course data, but the data are data for a human science not simply inasmuch as they are given but only inasmuch as there attaches to them some common-sense meaning. Thus, one could send into a law court as many physicists, chemists, and biologists as one pleased with as much equipment as they desired. They could count, measure, weigh, describe, record, analyse, dissect to their hearts' content. But it would be only by going beyond what is just given and by attending to the meaning of the proceedings that they could discover they were dealing with a court of law; and it is only insofar as the court of law is recognized as such and the appropriate meanings are attached to the sounds and actions that the data for a human science emerge.

A further consequence has to be noted. Precisely because everyday, common-sense meaning is constitutive of the data of a human science, phenomenology and hermeneutics and history assume basic importance. Phenomenology interprets our posture and movements, our acts and deeds. Hermeneutics interprets our words. History makes us aware that human meanings change with place and time. Clearly such an emphasis on meaning and such elaborate techniques for the study of meanings greatly reduce the relevance of counting, measuring, correlating and so move the *Geisteswissenschaften* away from the ambit of natural science and towards a close connection with—or a strong reaction against—idealist, historicist, phenomenological, personalist, or existentialist thought.

I am indicating, of course, no more than broad tendencies. Sigmund Freud interpreted meanings but, although he was a Viennese, he did so in terms of a primary process modelled on energy accumulation and discharge.[3] In contrast, a group of American social scientists defined the orientation of action by the meaning which the actor attaches to it.[4] And while we have thoroughgoing behaviorists for whom, even when awake, we are somnambulists,[5] there is also a third force in psychology that avows the insufficiency both of Freud and of straightforward experimentalists.[6] In brief, the point I am attempting to make in no way is a contrast between peoples or nations. Rather it has to do with a radical dilemma in modern culture. Is science to be conceived and worked out in total independence of philosophy or is it not?

Historically, then, modern science grew out of an opposition to Aristotle. Further, its development and its success are to a great extent due to the ground rule of the Royal Society that excluded from consideration questions that could not be settled by an appeal to observation or experiment. Finally, philosophy is not the name of some one thing, such as are physics, chemistry, biology. On the contrary, it is the name of a shifting multitude of conflicting things. At least, until philosophers reach, if not agreement, then comprehensiveness in their disagreements, it would be suicidal for scientists not to insist on their autonomy.

Still, this is only one side of the picture. For the moment the scientist ceases to speak of the objects in his field and begins to speak of his science itself, he is subscribing to some account of human cognitional activity, to some view of the relation between such activity and its objects, to some opinion on the possible objects to be reached through that relation. Whether he knows it or not, whether he admits it or not, he is talking cognitional theory, epistemology, and metaphysics.[7] Molière depicted the *médecin malgré lui*, the doctor despite himself. The modern scientist with a claim to complete autonomy is the *philosophe malgré lui*.

I have been attempting to characterize the reflexive, objectifying superstructure in modern culture, and I may now draw closer to my topic and observe that the modern notion of science tends to replace theology, which treats of God and all other things in their relation to God, with religious studies, which treat of man in his supposed dealings with God or gods or goddesses.

For a modern science is an empirical one. Whether it studies nature or man, whether it is oriented by behaviorism or by the *Geisteswissenschaften*, it begins from data, it discerns intelligible unities and relationships within data, and it is subject to the check of verification, to the correction and revision to be effected by confrontation with further relevant data. Now such procedures cannot lead one beyond this world. The divine is not a datum to be observed by sense or to be uncovered by introspection. Nor will any intelligible unity or relationship verifiable within such data lead us totally beyond such data to God. Precisely because modern science is specialized knowledge of man and of nature, it cannot include knowledge of God. God is neither man nor nature. It would only be the idolatry of identifying God with man or with nature if one attempted to know God through the methods of modern science.

Religion, however, is very human. So we have histories of

religion, phenomenologies of religion, psychologies of religion, sociologies of religion, philosophies of religion, and, to unite these many parts into a whole, the science of religion. These disciplines cannot, of course, escape the radical dilemma confronting modern science. In the measure they follow the model provided by natural science, they tend toward a reductionism that empties human living and especially human religion of all serious content. In the measure they insist on their specific difference from the natural sciences, they risk losing their autonomy and becoming the captive of some fashion or fad in philosophy. But whichever way they tend, at least this much is certain: they cannot make scientific statements about God. As long as they remain within the boundaries specified by the methods of a modern science, they cannot get beyond describing and explaining the multiplicity and the variety of human religious attitudes.

God, then, is absent from modern science. Even the modern science of religion, though it bears witness to the divine, speaks not of God but of man. This, of course, is simply the inevitable result of specialization, of distinguishing different fields of investigation, of working out appropriate methods in each field, and of excluding conflicts of methodological precepts by pursuing different subjects separately. In the writings of St. Anselm there is no systematic distinction between theology and philosophy, and so his ontological argument is not what later would be desired, a strictly philosophic argument. In the writings of St. Thomas philosophy and theology are distinguished, but the distinction does not lead to a separation; so his celebrated five ways occur within a theological *Summa*. With Descartes occurs the effort to provide philosophy with its proper and independent foundations, and so not only to distinguish but also separate philosophy and theology. Still, Descartes did not attempt to separate philosophy and science; on the contrary, he attempted to prove the conservation of momentum by appealing to the immutability of God. Such a separation was effected materially when Newton did for mechanics what Euclid had done for geometry. It was effected formally by the rule that, if a hypothesis is not verifiable, it is not scientific.

But if increasing specialization prevents modern science from speaking of God, one would expect it to enable modern theology to speak of God all the more fully and effectively. However, while I hope and labor that this will be so, I have to grant that it is not yet achieved. Contemporary theology and especially contemporary Catholic theology are in a feverish ferment. An old theology is being recognized as obsolete. There is a scattering of new theological fragments. But a new integration—and by this I mean, not another integration of the old type, but a new type of integration—is not yet plainly in sight. Let me describe the situation briefly under five headings.

First, the modern science or discipline of religious studies has undercut the assumptions and antiquated the methods of a theology structured by Melchior Cano's *De locis theologicis*. Such a theology was classicist in its assumptions. Truth is eternal. Principles are immutable. Change is accidental. But religious studies deal meticulously with endless matters of detail. They find that the expressions of truth and the enunciations of principles are neither eternal nor immutable. They concentrate on the historical process in which these changes occur. They bring to light whole ranges of interesting facts and quite new types of problem. In brief, religious studies have stripped the old theology of its very sources in scripture, in patristic writings, in medieval and subsequent religious writers. They have done so by subjecting the sources to a fuller and more penetrating scrutiny than had been attempted by earlier methods.

Secondly, there is the new demythologization of scripture. The old demythologization took place at the end of the second century. It consisted in rejecting the Bible's anthropomorphic conception of God. It may be summed up in Clement of Alexandria's statement: "Even though it is written, one must not so much as think of the Father of all as having a shape, as moving, as standing or seated or in a place, as having a right hand or a left." [8] Now to this old philosophic critique of biblical statement there has been added a literary and historical critique that

171

poses radical questions about the composition of the Gospels, about the infancy narratives, the miracle stories, the sayings attributed to Jesus, the accounts of His resurrection, the origins of Pauline and Joannine *theologoumena.*

Thirdly, there is the thrust of modern philosophy. Theologians not only repeat the past but also speak to people of today. The old theology was content, for the most part, to operate with technical concepts derived from Greek and medieval thought. But the concreteness of modern science has imposed a similar concreteness on much modern philosophy. Historicism, phenomenology, personalism, existentialism belong to a climate utterly different from that of the *per se* subject with his necessary principles or processes and his claims to demonstration. Moreover, this movement of philosophy towards concreteness and especially to the concreteness of human living has brought to light a host of notions, approaches, procedures, that are proving very fertile and illuminating in theology.

Fourthly, there is the collapse of Thomism. In the thirties it seemed still in the ascendent. After the war it seemed for a while to be holding its ground. Since Vatican II it seems to have vanished. Aquinas still is a great and venerated figure in the history of Catholic thought. But Aquinas no longer is thought of or appealed to as an arbiter in contemporary Catholic thought. Nor is the sudden change really surprising. For the assumption, on which Thomism rested was typically classicist. It supposed the existence of a single perennial philosophy that might need to be adapted in this or that accidental detail but in substance remained the repository of human wisdom, a permanent oracle, and, like Thucydides' history, a possession for all time. In fact, there are a perennial materialism and a perennial idealism as well as a perennial realism. They all shift and change from one age to the next, for the questions they once treated become obsolete and the methods they employed are superseded.

Fifthly, there is a notable softening, if not weakening, of the dogmatic component once so prominent in Catholic theology. Nor can this be described as simply the correction of a former exaggeration, the advent of charity, ecumenism, dialogue, in place of less pleasant attitudes. The new philosophies are not

172

capable of grounding objective statements about what really is so. But dogmas purport to be such objective statements. Accordingly, if one is to defend dogmas as meaningful, one has to get beyond historicism, phenomenology, personalism, existentialism. One has to meet head on the contention that the only meaningful statements are either scientific or mythical statements. One has to do so not partially and fragmentarily but completely and thoroughly.

Further it is not only dogmas that are at stake, for it is not only dogmas that lie outside the range of modern science. Not only every statement about God but also every statement about scientific method, about hermeneutics, about historiography supposes a reflexive procedure quite distinct from the direct procedures sanctioned by the success of modern science.

To conclude, Catholic theology at present is at a critical juncture. If I may express a personal view, I should say that the contemporary task of assimilating the fruits both of religious studies and of the new philosophies, of handling the problems of demythologization and of the possibility of objective religious statement, imposes on theology the task of recasting its notion of theological method in the most thoroughgoing and profound fashion.

I have been speaking, not of the whole of modern culture, not of its most vital part, but of its superstructure. I have said that God is absent from modern science precisely because such science systematically and exclusively is directed to knowledge of this world. Further I have said that Catholic theology is going through an unsettling period of transition in which older procedures are being repudiated and newer ones yield only incomplete and fragmentary benefits. But I have yet to ask whether God is absent not from the superstructure of modern culture but from the everyday, familiar domain of feeling, insight, judgment, decision.

On this more concrete level modern culture involves a reinterpretation of man and his world, a transformation of the ordering of society and of the control over nature, and a new sense of power and of responsibility. All three have a bearing on the absence of God in modern culture.

First, there is the reinterpretation of man in his world. This reinterpretation primarily occurs in the cultural superstructure, in the natural and the human sciences, in philosophy, history, and theology. But it is not confined to the superstructure. It is popularized, schematized, simplified. It is transposed from technical statement through simile and metaphor, image and narrative, catch-phrase and slogan, to what can be understood without too much effort and is judged to be, for practical purposes, sufficiently accurate.

Now it is quite conceivable that in a process of great cultural change all parts of the superstructure should keep in step and the popularizations of the several parts should be coherent. Such, however, has not been the transition from classicist to modern culture. For, in the first place, the classicist believed that he could escape history, that he could encapsulate culture in the universal, the normative, the ideal, the immutable, that, while times would change, still the changes necessarily would be minor, accidental, of no serious significance. In the second place, the classicist judged modern science in the light of the Aristotelian notion of science and by that standard found it wanting, for modern science does not proceed from self-evident, necessary principles and it does not demonstrate conclusions from such principles. In the third place, classicist churchmen found that the natural sciences frequently were presented in a reductionist version that was materialistic and, if not atheistic, at least agnostic, while the historical sciences were the locus of continuous attacks on traditional views of the Church in its origins and throughout its development. In brief, so far were churchmen from acknowledging the distinctive character of modern culture that they regarded it as an aberration that had to be resisted and overcome. When they were confronted with a heresy, which they considered to be the sum and substance of all heresy, they named it modernism. So far were they from seeking to enrich modern culture with a religious interpretation that they had only mistrust for a Pierre Teilhard de Chardin.

Today the pendulum has swung to the opposite extreme. Whatever is old, is out. Whatever is new, is in. But a mere swing of the pendulum, while it involves plently of novelty, falls far short of *aggiornamento*. For *aggiornamento* is not some simple-minded rejection of all that is old and some breezy acceptance of everything new. Rather it is a disengagement from a culture that no longer exists and an involvement in a distinct culture that has replaced it. Christians have been depicted as utterly other-worldly, as idly standing about awaiting the second coming of Christ without any interest or concern or commitment for the things of this life of ours on earth. But the fact of the matter is that the ancient Church went about transforming Greek and Roman culture, that the medieval Church was a principal agent in the formation of medieval culture, that the Renaissance Church was scandalously involved in Renaissance culture. If the modern Church has stood aloof from the modern world, the fact is not too hard to explain. On the one hand, the Church's involvement in classicist culture was an involvement in a very limited view that totally underestimated the possibilities of cultural change and so precluded advertence to the need for adaptation and zeal to effect it. On the other hand, modern culture with its many excellences and its unprecedented achievements none the less is not just a realm of sweetness and light. The suffering, the sins, the crimes, the destructive power, the sustained blindness of the twentieth century have disenchanted us with progress and made us suspicious of development and advance. *Aggiornamento* is not desertion of the past but only a discerning and discriminating disengagement from its limitations. *Aggiornamento* is not just acceptance of the present; it is acknowledgment of its evils as well as of its good; and, as acknowledgment alone is not enough, it also is, by the power of the Cross, that meeting of evil with good that transforms evil into good.

Besides its reinterpretation of man in his world, modern culture transforms man's control over nature and in consequence involves a reordering of society. The new scene is one of technology, automation, built-in obsolescence, a population explosion, increasing longevity, urbanism, mobility, detached and functional relations between persons, universal, prolonged, and continuing education, increasing leisure and travel, instantaneous information, and perpetually available entertainment. In this ever-changing scene God, when not totally absent, appears an intruder. To mention Him, if not meaningless, seems to be irrelevant. The greatest of financial powers, the power to increase gross national income by taxing and spending for worthy purposes, is restricted to non-religious ends, so that pluralism is given lip-service while secularism is the religion—or, perhaps, the anti-religion—by law established. At the same time, a rigorously codified religious organization finds itself ever less capable to move with ever fluid situations, to enter meaningfully into people's lives, significantly to further all good causes, effectively to help the weak, heal the hurt, restore and reinvigorate the disheartened. Here, perhaps, as Karl Rahner has argued, the difficulty has been an integrism, in the sense that it was believed possible for authority to solve problems by laying down principles and deducing conclusions. However true such principles, however accurate such conclusions may be, it remains that they can become relevant to concrete situations only through familiarity with the situation, only through adequate insight into its causes and its potentialities, only through the ingenuity that discovers lines of solution and keeps developing and adapting them in accord with an on-going process of change. Once more, then, we have to move beyond the classicist position and operate in the modern world. Ideals and principles and exhortations have not been antiquated. But the crying need is for the competent man on the spot, free to deal with real issues as they arise and develop.

Besides a reinterpretation of man in his world, a transformation of man's control over nature and a consequent reordering of society, modern culture has generated a new sense of power and responsibility. Superficially the sense of power might be illustrated by space-exploration, and the sense of responsibility by concern over nuclear bombs. But the matter goes far deeper. Modern culture is the culture that knows about itself and other cultures. It is aware that they are man-made. It is aware that the cultural may sustain or destroy or refashion the social. So it is that modern man not only individually is responsible for the life he leads but also collectively is responsible

for the world in which he leads it. So modern culture is culture
on the move. It is not dedicated to perpetuating the wisdom of
ancestors, to handing on the traditions it has inherited. The
past is just the springboard to the future. It is the set of good
things to be improved and of evils to be eliminated. The future
will belong to those who think about it, who grasp real possibilities, who project a coherent sequence of cumulative realizations, who speak to man's longing for achievement more
wisely than the liberal apostles of automatic progress and more
humanly than the liquidating Marxists.

Now this concern with the future of humanity is a concern
for humanity in this world and so it has been thought to be
purely secular. Such a conclusion is, I believe, mistaken. It is
true that concern for the future is incompatible with a blind
traditionalism, but a blind traditionalism is not the essence of
religion. It is true that concern for the future will work itself
out by human means, by drawing on human experience, human
intelligence, human judgment, human decision, but again this
is quite compatible with a profoundly religious attitude. It was
St. Ignatius Loyola who gave the advice: Act as though results
depended exclusively on you, but await the results as though
they depended entirely on God. What is false is that human
concern for the future can generate a better future on the
basis of individual and group egoism. For to know what is truly
good and to effect it calls for a self-transcendence that seeks
to benefit not self at the cost of the group, not the group at
the cost of mankind, not present mankind at the cost of mankind's future. Concern for the future, if it is not just high-
sounding hypocrisy, supposes rare moral attainment. It calls
for what Christians name heroic charity. In the measure that
Christians practice and radiate heroic charity they need not
fear they will be superfluous either in the task of discerning
man's true good in this life or in the task of bringing it about.

I have been speaking of the absence of God in modern culture. I have dwelt at length on the many ways in which He is
absent both in the superstructure and on the day-to-day level
of that culture. But every absence is also a potential presence,
not indeed in the sense that the past is to be restored, but in the

The Contemporary Problem of God

sense that our creativity has to discover the future and our determination has to realize it. Nor is God's presence only potential. Evidently, almost palpably, it is actual. Pope John spoke to the whole world. Vatican II stirred it profoundly. For the Spirit of God is moving the hearts of many and, in Paul Tillich's phrase, ultimate concern has grasped them.

NOTES

1. E. Rothacker, *Systematik und Logik der Geisteswissenschaften* (Bonn, 1947).
2. H. Butterfield, *The Origins of Modern Science, 1300–1800*, Revised edition (New York: Free Press, 1965), p. 7.
3. See Joseph Nuttin, "Human Motivation and Freud's Theory of Energy Discharge," in Irwin Sarason (ed.), *Science and Theory in Psychoanalysis* (Princeton: Van Nostrand, 1965). Also Paul Ricoeur, *De l'interprétation, essai sur Freud* (Paris: Seuil, 1965).
4. Talcott Parsons and Edward A. Shils (ed.), *Toward a General Theory of Action* (New York: Harper and Row, 1965), p. 4.
5. F. W. Matson, *The Broken Image* (New York: Doubleday, 1964), pp. 38–65.
6. See Abraham Maslow, *Toward a Psychology of Being* (Princeton: Van Nostrand, 1962).
7. For a distinction between the scientific and the philosophic elements in the Principle of Complementarity, see Patrick Heelan, *Quantum Mechanics and Objectivity* (The Hague: Martinus Nijhoff, 1965), pp. 55–80.
8. Clemens Alexandrinus, *Stromateis* V, 11; 71. 4 (G.C.S. edit. Stählin, II, 374). PG 9, 110 a.